Modern Critical Interpretations

Eugene O'Neill's
Long Day's Journey into Night

Modern Critical Interpretations

These and other titles in preparation

Eugene O'Neill's
Long Day's Journey into Night

Edited and with an introduction by

Harold Bloom
Sterling Professor of the Humanities
Yale University

Chelsea House Publishers
NEW YORK ◊ PHILADELPHIA

© 1987 by Chelsea House Publishers, a division of Main Line
Book Co.

Introduction © 1987 by Harold Bloom

Printed and bound in the United States of America

10 9 8 7 6 5 4 3 2

∞ The paper used in this publication meets the minimum
requirements of the American National Standard for Permanence
of Paper for Printed Library Materials, Z39.48-1984.

Library of Congress Cataloging-in-Publication Data

Eugene O'Neill's Long day's journey into night.
    (Modern critical interpretations)
    Bibliography: p.
    Includes index.
    Summary: A collection of ten critical essays on
O'Neill's play, arranged in chronological order of
their original publication.
    1. O'Neill, Eugene, 1888–1953. Long day's journey
into night. [1. O'Neill, Eugene, 1888–1953. Long
day's journey into night.   2. American literature—
History and criticism]   I. Bloom, Harold.   II. Series.
PS3529.N5L6   1987   812'.52   86–29942
ISBN 1-55546-049-6 (alk. paper)

Contents

Editor's Note

This book brings together what I judge to be the most useful criticism available upon Eugene O'Neill's masterwork, *Long Day's Journey into Night*, with the essays reprinted here in the chronological order of their original publication. I am grateful to John Rogers for his skilled work of research in connection with this volume.

My introduction speculates on the relation of O'Neill to American literary and cultural tradition, and then attempts an estimate of both the strength and limits of *Long Day's Journey*. Doris V. Falk begins the chronological sequence of criticism with her early estimate, which regards the play as essentially nihilistic. The emphasis is very different in Robert Brustein's remarks, which characterize *Long Day's Journey* as an "existential rebellion." Raymond Williams regards the drama as a final playing-out of the naturalistic theatre of Ibsen and Strindberg, while Timo Tiusanen sees the naturalistic tradition yielding here to the power of dramatic monologue.

Egil Törnqvist centers upon the representation of forces and drives, as compared to that of persons, in the play. Two significant dramatic images, door and mirror, are explicated by Travis Bogard, while Jean Chothia explores *Long Day's Journey* as an integration of the verbal and visual levels of representation.

Working out of his profound knowledge of the literary genre of tragedy, Richard B. Sewall sees the drama as saved from mere sorrowfulness by its characters' capacity for learning from their own suffering. John Orr judges *Long Day's Journey* as surpassing the dark vision of Samuel Beckett, in a judgment that is interesting but certainly disputable.

In this book's final essay, the British critic C. W. E. Bigsby praises the play as O'Neill's achievement of a loss of self that was transcendence rather than death. I myself would conclude with the prophecy that O'Neill, and *Long Day's Journey* in particular, need a different kind of literary criticism of drama than anything we now have, a criticism that might be able to deal more adequately with O'Neill's eloquence of gestures and groupings, which seems to me so much more intense than his more limited rhetorical eloquence.

Introduction

It is an inevitable oddity that the principal American dramatist to date should have no American precursors. Eugene O'Neill's art as a playwright owes most to Strindberg's, and something crucial, though rather less, to Ibsen's. Intellectually, O'Neill's ancestry also has little to do with American tradition, with Emerson or William James or any other of our cultural speculators. Schopenhauer, Nietzsche, and Freud formed O'Neill's sense of what little was possible for any of us. Even where American literary tradition was strongest, in the novel and poetry, it did not much affect O'Neill. His novelists were Zola and Conrad; his poets were Dante Gabriel Rossetti and Swinburne. Overwhelmingly an Irish-American, with his Jansenist Catholicism transformed into anger at God, he had little active interest in the greatest American writer, Whitman, though his spiritual darkness has a curious, antithetical relation to Whitman's overt analysis of our national character.

Yet O'Neill, despite his many limitations, is the most American of our handful of dramatists who matter most: Williams, Miller, Wilder, Albee, perhaps Mamet and Shepard. A national quality that is literary, yet has no clear relation to our domestic literary traditions, is nearly always present in O'Neill's strongest works. We can recognize Hawthorne in Henry James, and Whitman (however repressed) in T. S. Eliot, while the relation of Hemingway and Faulkner to Mark Twain is just as evident as their debt to Conrad. Besides the question of his genre (since there was no vital American drama before O'Neill), there would seem to be some hidden factor that governed O'Neill's ambiguous relation to our literary past. It was certainly not the lack of critical discernment on O'Neill's part. His admiration for Hart Crane's poetry, at its most difficult, was solely responsible for the

1

publication of Crane's first volume, *White Buildings*, for which O'Neill initially offered to write the introduction, withdrawing in favor of Allen Tate when the impossibility of his writing a critical essay on Crane's complexities became clear to O'Neill. But to have recognized Hart Crane's genius, so early and so helpfully, testifies to O'Neill's profound insights into the American literary imagination at its strongest.

The dramatist whose masterpieces are *The Iceman Cometh* and *Long Day's Journey into Night*, and, in a class just short of those, *A Moon for the Misbegotten* and *A Touch of the Poet*, is not exactly to be regarded as a celebrator of the possibilities of American life. The central strain in our literature remains Emersonian, from Whitman to our contemporaries like Saul Bellow and John Ashbery. Even the tradition that reacted against Emerson—from Poe, Hawthorne, and Melville through Gnostics of the abyss like Nathanael West and Thomas Pynchon—remains always alert to transcendental and extraordinary American possibilities. Our most distinguished living writer, Robert Penn Warren, must be the most overtly anti-Emersonian partisan in our history, yet even Warren seeks an American Sublime in his still-ongoing poetry. O'Neill would appear to be the most non-Emersonian author of any eminence in our literature. Irish-American through and through, with an heroic resentment of the New England Yankee tradition, O'Neill from the start seemed to know that his spiritual quest was to undermine Emerson's American religion of self-reliance.

O'Neill's own Irish Jansenism is curiously akin to the New England Puritanism he opposed, but that only increased the rancor of his powerful polemic in *Desire under the Elms*, *Mourning Becomes Electra*, and *More Stately Mansions*. The Will to Live is set against New England Puritanism in what O'Neill himself once called "the battle of moral forces in the New England scene" to which he said he felt closest as an artist. But since this is Schopenhauer's rapacious Will to Live, and not Bernard Shaw's genial revision of that Will into the Life Force of a benign Creative Evolution, O'Neill is in the terrible position of opposing one death-drive with another. Only the inescapable Strindberg comes to mind as a visionary quite as negative as O'Neill, so that *The Iceman Cometh* might as well have been called *The Dance of Death*, and *Long Day's Journey into Night* could be retitled *The Ghost Sonata*. O'Neill's most powerful self-representations—as Edmund in *Long Day's Journey* and Larry Slade in *Iceman*—are astonishingly negative identifications, particularly in an American context.

Edmund and Slade do not long for death in the mode of Whitman and his descendants—Wallace Stevens, T. S. Eliot, Hart Crane, and Theodore Roethke—all of whom tend to incorporate the image of a desired death into the great, triple trope of night, the mother, and the sea. Edmund Tyrone and Larry Slade long to die because life without transcendence is impossible, and yet transcendence is totally unavailable. O'Neill's true polemic against his country and its spiritual tradition is not, as he insisted, that "its main idea is that everlasting game of trying to possess your own soul by the possession of something outside it." Though uttered in 1946, in remarks before the first performance of *The Iceman Cometh*, such a reflection is banal and represents a weak misreading of *The Iceman Cometh*. The play's true argument is that your own soul cannot be possessed, whether by possessing something or someone outside it, or by joining yourself to a transcendental possibility, to whatever version of an Emersonian Oversoul that you might prefer. The United States, in O'Neill's dark view, was uniquely the country that had refused to learn the truths of the spirit, which are that good and the means of good, love and the means of love, are irreconcilable.

Such a formulation is Shelleyan, and reminds one of O'Neill's High Romantic inheritance, which reached him through pre-Raphaelite poetry and literary speculation. O'Neill seems a strange instance of the Aestheticism of Rossetti and Pater, but his metaphysical nihilism, desperate faith in art, and phantasmagoric naturalism stem directly from them. When Jamie Tyrone quotes from Rossetti's "Willowwood" sonnets, he gives the epigraph not only to *Long Day's Journey* but to all of O'Neill: "Look into my face. My name is Might-Have-Been; / I am also called No More, Too Late, Farewell." In O'Neill's deepest polemic, the lines are quoted by, and for, all Americans of imagination whatsoever.

II

By common consent, *Long Day's Journey into Night* is Eugene O'Neill's masterpiece. The Yale paperback in which I have just reread the play lists itself as the fifty-sixth printing in the thirty years since publication. Since O'Neill, rather than Williams or Miller, Wilder or Albee, is recognized as our leading dramatist, *Long Day's Journey* must be the best play in our more than two centuries as a nation. One rereads it therefore with awe and a certain apprehension, but with considerable puzzlement also. Strong work it certainly is, and twice I have been moved by watching it well directed and well performed. Yet how can this be the best stage play that an exuberantly dramatic people has produced? Is it equal to the best of our imaginative literature? Can we read it in the company of *The Scarlet Letter* and *Moby-Dick*, *Adventures of Huckleberry Finn* and *The Portrait of a Lady*, *As I*

Lay Dying and *Gravity's Rainbow*? Does it have the aesthetic distinction of our greatest poets, of Whitman, Dickinson, Frost, Stevens, Eliot, Hart Crane, Elizabeth Bishop, and John Ashbery? Can it stand intellectually with the crucial essays of Emerson and of William James?

These questions, alas, are self-answering. O'Neill's limitations are obvious and need not be surveyed intensively. Perhaps no major dramatist has ever been so lacking in rhetorical exuberance, in what Yeats once praised Blake for having: "beautiful, laughing speech." O'Neill's convictions were deeply held, but were in no way remarkable, except for their incessant sullenness. It is embarrassing when O'Neill's exegetes attempt to expound his ideas, whether about his country, his own work, or the human condition. When one of them speaks of "two kinds of nonverbal, tangential poetry in *Long Day's Journey into Night*" as the characters' longing "for a mystical union of sorts," and the influence of the setting, I am compelled to reflect that insofar as O'Neill's art is nonverbal it must also be nonexistent.

My reflection however is inaccurate, and O'Neill's dramatic art is considerable, though it does make us revise our notions of just how strictly literary an art drama necessarily has to be. Sophocles, Shakespeare, and Molière are masters alike of language and of a mimetic force that works through gestures that supplement language, but O'Neill is mastered by language and relies instead upon a drive-towards-staging that he appears to have learned from Strindberg. Consider the close of *Long Day's Journey.* How much of the power here comes from what Tyrone and Mary say, and how much from the extraordinarily effective stage directions?

> TYRONE (*trying to shake off his hopeless stupor*). Oh, we're fools to pay any attention. It's the damned poison. But I've never known her to drown herself in it as deep as this. (*Gruffly.*) Pass me that bottle, Jamie. And stop reciting that damned morbid poetry. I won't have it in my house! (*Jamie pushes the bottle toward him. He pours a drink without disarranging the wedding gown he holds carefully over his other arm and on his lap, and shoves the bottle back. Jamie pours his and passes the bottle to Edmund, who, in turn, pours one. Tyrone lifts his glass and his sons follow suit mechanically, but before they can drink Mary speaks and they slowly lower their drinks to the table, forgetting them.*)
>
> MARY (*staring dreamily before her. Her face looks extraordinarily youthful and innocent. The shyly eager, trusting smile is on her lips as she talks aloud to herself*). I had a talk with Mother Elizabeth. She is so sweet and good. A saint on earth. I love her dearly. It may be sinful of me but I love her better than my

own mother. Because she always understands, even before you say a word. Her kind blue eyes look right into your heart. You can't keep any secrets from her. You couldn't deceive her, even if you were mean enough to want to. (*She gives a little rebellious toss of her head—with girlish pique.*) All the same, I don't think she was so understanding this time. I told her I wanted to be a nun. I explained how sure I was of my vocation, that I had prayed to the Blessed Virgin to make me sure, and to find me worthy. I told Mother I had had a true vision when I was praying in the shrine of Our Lady of Lourdes, on the little island in the lake. I said I knew, as surely as I knew I was kneeling there, that the Blessed Virgin had smiled and blessed me with her consent. But Mother Elizabeth told me I must be more sure than that, even, that I must prove it wasn't simply my imagination. She said, if I was so sure, then I wouldn't mind putting myself to a test by going home after I graduated, and living as other girls lived, going out to parties and dances and enjoying myself; and then if after a year or two I still felt sure, I could come back to see her and we would talk it over again. (*She tosses her head—indignantly.*) I never dreamed Holy Mother would give me such advice! I was really shocked. I said, of course, I would do anything she suggested, but I knew it was simply a waste of time. After I left her, I felt all mixed up, so I went to the shrine and prayed to the Blessed Virgin and found peace again because I knew she heard my prayer and would always love me and see no harm ever came to me so long as I never lost my faith in her. (*She pauses and a look of growing uneasiness comes over her face. She passes a hand over her forehead as if brushing cobwebs from her brain—vaguely.*) That was in the winter of senior year. Then in the spring something happened to me. Yes, I remember. I fell in love with James Tyrone and was so happy for a time. (*She stares before her in a sad dream. Tyrone stirs in his chair. Edmund and Jamie remain motionless.*)

CURTAIN

Critics have remarked on how fine it is that the three alcoholic Tyrone males slowly lower their drinks to the table, forgetting them, as the morphine-laden wife and mother begins to speak. One can go further; her banal if moving address to herself, and Tyrone's petulant outbursts, are considerably less eloquent than the stage directions. I had not remembered anything that was spoken, returning to the text after a decade, but I had held on to that grim family tableau of the three Tyrones slowly lowering their glasses. Again, I had remembered nothing actually said between Edmund and his mother at the end of act one, but the gestures and glances between them always abide with me, and Mary's reactions when she is left alone compel in me the Nietzschean realization that the truly memorable is always associated with what is most painful.

> (*She puts her arms around him and hugs him with a frightened, protective tenderness.*)
>
> EDMUND (*soothingly*). That's foolishness. You know it's only a bad cold.
>
> MARY. Yes, of course, I know that!
>
> EDMUND. But listen, Mama. I want you to promise me that even if it should turn out to be something worse, you'll know I'll soon be all right again, anyway, and you won't worry yourself sick, and you'll keep on taking care of yourself—
>
> MARY (*frightenedly*). I won't listen when you're so silly! There's absolutely no reason to talk as if you expected something dreadful! Of course, I promise you. I give you my sacred word of honor! (*Then with a sad bitterness.*) But I suppose you're remembering I've promised before on my word of honor.
>
> EDMUND. No!
>
> MARY (*her bitterness receding into a resigned helplessness*). I'm not blaming you, dear. How can you help it? How can any one of us forget? (*Strangely.*) That's what makes it so hard—for all of us. We can't forget.
>
> EDMUND (*grabs her shoulder*). Mama! Stop it!
>
> MARY (*forcing a smile*). All right, dear. I didn't mean to be so gloomy. Don't mind me. Here. Let me feel your head. Why, it's nice and cool. You certainly haven't any fever now.
>
> EDMUND. Forget! It's you—
>
> MARY. But I'm quite all right, dear. (*With a quick, strange, calculating, almost sly glance at him.*) Except I naturally feel tired and nervous this morning, after such a bad night. I really ought to go upstairs and lie down until lunch time and take a nap. (*He gives her an instinctive look of suspicion—then,*

> *ashamed of himself, looks quickly away. She hurries on nervously.*)
> What are you going to do? Read here? It would be much
> better for you to go out in the fresh air and sunshine. But
> don't get overheated, remember. Be sure and wear a hat.
> (*She stops, looking straight at him now. He avoids her eyes. There
> is a tense pause. Then she speaks jeeringly.*) Or are you afraid to
> trust me alone?
>
> EDMUND (*tormentedly*). No! Can't you stop talking like that! I
> think you ought to take a nap. (*He goes to the screen door—
> forcing a joking tone.*) I'll go down and help Jamie bear up. I
> love to lie in the shade and watch him work. (*He forces a
> laugh in which she makes herself join. Then he goes out on the
> porch and disappears down the steps. Her first reaction is one of
> relief. She appears to relax. She sinks down in one of the wicker
> armchairs at rear of table and leans her head back, closing her eyes.
> But suddenly she grows terribly tense again. Her eyes open and she
> strains forward, seized by a fit of nervous panic. She begins a des-
> perate battle with herself. Her long fingers, warped and knotted by
> rheumatism, drum on the arms of the chair, driven by an insistent
> life of their own, without her consent.*)
>
> CURTAIN

That grim ballet of looks between mother and son, followed by
the terrible, compulsive drumming of her long fingers, has a lyric force
that only the verse quotations from Baudelaire, Swinburne, and others in
O'Neill's text are able to match. Certainly a singular dramatic genius is
always at work in O'Neill's stage directions, and can be felt also, most
fortunately, in the repressed intensities of inarticulateness in all of the
Tyrones.

It seems to me a marvel that this can suffice, and in itself probably it
could not. But there is also O'Neill's greatest gift, more strongly present in
Long Day's Journey than it is even in *The Iceman Cometh*. Lionel Trilling,
subtly and less equivocally than it seemed, once famously praised Theodore
Dreiser for his mixed but imposing representation of "reality in America,"
in his best novels, *Sister Carrie* and *An American Tragedy*. One cannot deny the
power of the mimetic art of *Long Day's Journey into Night*. No dramatist to
this day, among us, has matched O'Neill in depicting the nightmare realities
that can afflict American family life, indeed family life in the twentieth-
century Western world. And yet that is the authentic subject of our dramatists who matter most after O'Neill: Williams, Miller, Albee, with the
genial Thornton Wilder as the grand exception. It is a terrifying distinction

that O'Neill earns, and more decisively in *Long Day's Journey into Night* than anywhere else. He is the elegist of the Freudian "family romance," of the domestic tragedy of which we all die daily, a little bit at a time. The helplessness of family love to sustain, let alone heal, the wounds of marriage, of parenthood, and of sonship, have never been so remorselessly and so pathetically portrayed, and with a force of gesture too painful ever to be forgotten by any of us.

*L*ong Day's Journey

Doris V. Falk

In 1941 O'Neill completed *Long Day's Journey into Night*. A few of his close friends were permitted to read the manuscript, but the author stipulated that the play was not to be produced or published until twenty-five years after his death. Copies were placed in the vaults of O'Neill's publisher, Random House, and in the Yale University Library (along with early drafts and notes). When reporters at the *Iceman* interview had asked him to explain the restriction, O'Neill had answered, "There is one person in it who is still alive." In February of 1956, however, three years after O'Neill's death, *Long Day's Journey* was published with Mrs. O'Neill's permission. According to the *New York Times* of February 19, 1956, Random House considered O'Neill's twenty-five-year restriction still valid and canceled its contract rather than publish. Yale University Press published the play and said in a subsequent letter to the *Times*:

> American and Canadian publication rights in the play were given by Mr. O'Neill's widow, Carlotta Monterey O'Neill to the Yale University Library. . . . Having been assured that the playwright had lifted his original restriction concerning the publication of the play, the Library arranged for its publication. All royalties from the sale of the book under the terms of the deed of gift are to be paid to Yale University to set up an endowed Eugene O'Neill Memorial Fund.

From *Eugene O'Neill and the Tragic Tension: An Interpretive Study of the Plays.* © 1958 by Rutgers, The State University. Rutgers University Press, 1958.

Long Day's Journey was performed in Stockholm even before the published play appeared on the American market. O'Neill had left it, evidently, as "a deathbed legacy to a nation which he felt had been more loyal to him than his own" (*Newsweek*, International Edition, February 20, 1956). Its reception was immediately enthusiastic. One Swedish critic, quoted in *Newsweek*, described the play as "one of the most powerful realistic dramas of the century. It's Ibsen's dramatic technique, but without his . . . symbolical overemphasis."

The critic hit home. *Long Day's Journey* is excruciatingly powerful because it is so painfully and consistently realistic. That is not intended to imply that literal realism is generally a criterion of dramatic power, but only that it frequently is in O'Neill's work, where realism is so often lost among unintegrated symbols, O'Neill's attempt at poetry. In *Long Day's Journey* when the elder Tyrone (James O'Neill, Sr.) tells his son Edmund (Eugene) that he has the "makings of a poet," Edmund replies that he hasn't even the makings. "I just stammered. That's the best I'll ever do. . . . Well, it will be faithful realism at least. Stammering is the native eloquence of us fog people." And in *Long Day's Journey* the inarticulate child of fog speaks with his native eloquence.

For all its realism the play is full of symbols. The fog was O'Neill's first and last symbol of man's inability to know himself, or other men, or his destiny. In act 1 of *Long Day's Journey* the sun is shining; in act 2 the haze gathers; in act 3 a wall of fog stands thick against the windowpanes. Through the fog at intervals a foghorn moans, followed by a warning chorus of ship's bells—the leitmotif of the family fate, sounding whenever that fate asserts itself.

The interior set has its symbolic value too. The curtain rises on "the living room of James Tyrone's summer house in a morning in August, 1912. At rear are two double doorways with portieres. The one at the right leads into a front parlor with the formally arranged, set appearance of a room rarely occupied. The other opens on a dark, windowless back parlor, never used except as a passageway from living room to dining room." All the visible action takes place before these doorways, in a shabby, cheaply furnished living room lined with well-used books, the titles of which are largely those of O'Neill's acknowledged influences. The family "lives" in that mid-region between the bright formality of the exterior front parlor— the mask—and the little-known dark of the rear room.

In that living room the four Tyrones torment themselves and each other, gradually stripping away every protective illusion until at the end each character must face himself and the others without hope, but with a measure of tolerance and pity. The focal point of the play is the drug addiction of the mother and the family's early hope that she has been cured. As this "pipe dream" vanishes, the truths about the family emerge in anguished sequence. Each confession elicits another confession, but in spite of these often long and repetitious speeches the conflicts of hate and love, guilt and accusation, lead to tense, exhausting, and brilliant drama. The driving force of the family fate hurtles each of the characters into his own night and causes him to take the others with him. All the Tyrones are doomed to destroy and be destroyed, to be victimized not only by each other but by the dead, for the dead have willed them a heritage of disease, alcoholism, and drug addiction, and have cursed them with the deeper ills of alienation, conflict, and self-destructiveness.

This is O'Neill's own family, and their story was torn from the depths of his consciousness. With an effort compounded of "tears and blood," O'Neill forced himself to examine them honestly and objectively, from their own points of view as well as his. The result was that the figures most deeply rooted in that consciousness have emerged from it not simply as symbols of their meaning to the author, but as memorable, fully created individual personalities. But in each of these full portraits lurks the outline of a psychological type who has appeared and reappeared in O'Neill's work. Each type with its problems dominated a period in O'Neill's development, but there are only four Tyrones, and there are more than four stages in O'Neill's own journey into night; the other stages are to be found in the themes of this play and in O'Neill's very compulsion to write it.

Just as O'Neill's life journey began with his mother, his mature literary career began with "the searchers," those characters in his plays who were her direct descendants. Mary appears throughout the plays in two guises: what she was, and what her sons wanted her to be. She is the "eternal girl-woman," the wife and mother who longs to return (as in *Long Day's Journey* she does, in her drug fantasies) to the innocence of childhood and virginity. In *The Great God Brown* she was Dion's mother, whom he remembered as "a sweet, strange girl, with affectionate, bewildered eyes as if God had locked her in a dark closet without any explanation. . . . I watched her die with the shy pride of one who has lengthened her dress and put up her hair. . . . The last time I looked, her purity had forgotten me, she was stainless and imperishable, and I knew my sobs were ugly and meaningless to her virginity."

Mary is also the inverse image of the Earth Mother for whom her sons long. Her hair was once the same "rare shade of reddish-brown," which symbolized prenatal freedom, security, and warmth in *Mourning Becomes Electra*; but Mary cannot give her sons this peace, and her hair is white. She is aware of her failure, and constantly apologizes for the whiteness and disorder of her hair. It represents not only age but guilt, for the graying began with her drug addiction, after the birth of Edmund. She knows that Edmund has inherited from her his extreme sensitivity, his "nervousness" and fear of life —and through her, from her father, his susceptibility to tuberculosis. Edmund inherits from her also her sense of Fate, her awareness of the fog, with her momentary attempts to see through it— but alas, she has misplaced her glasses.

Mary's blindness is that of the protagonists of O'Neill's earliest full-length plays, written in the years before 1919. Like Mary, the searchers are aliens from self, seeking for meaning and identity—but whenever they approach the truth about themselves they must run away, back to the fog, where, alone, they can "belong." Mary tells her son, "I really love fog . . . it hides you from the world and the world from you. . . . It's the foghorn that I hate. It won't let you alone. It keeps reminding you, and warning you, and calling you back" (act 3). Edmund, too, the young O'Neill, longs for that mysterious region where self was lost and the tormenting masks of self can be lost again. He goes for a walk in the fog because "The fog was where I wanted to be. . . . Everything looked and sounded unreal. Nothing was what it is. . . . Who wants to see life as it is, if they can help it? It's the three Gorgons in one. You look in their faces and turn to stone. Or it's Pan. You see him and you die" (act 4).

Mary describes the fate of all the searchers when she says "None of us can help the things life has done to us. They're done before you realize it, and once they're done they make you do other things until at last everything comes between you and what you'd like to be, and you've lost your true self forever" (2.1). Ultimately, of course, this describes the fate of most of O'Neill's characters, but it is most precisely and pointedly applicable to the protagonists of the plays from *Beyond the Horizon* to *Anna Christie*. In the fog of their past mistakes they grope for themselves as Mary does, and they see dimly the Gorgon and the Pan—the opposite masks of death and life —which they must face in order to survive. Like Mary, they vacillate between love and hate, a longing for companionship and a longing for privacy, for sexual fulfillment and for purity. Mary was a dreamer, and so were her son and all his searchers. They cling to their idealism and their hopeless hope, and they catch a glimpse of one vision which O'Neill never completely lost—the idea that the eternal seeker and idealist in man struggles to overcome the limitations of self, to make the "mystery behind things" express *him*. This is a tragic effort, doomed to failure, but it is all that can give value to the searchers' lives. For most of the searchers, however, the vision is only momentary; they remain, like Mary, lost and alienated somewhere between the self that limits and the self that aspires.

This bewildered, submissive mother was, of course, only one of the images by which O'Neill was haunted. The dominant image for the fanatics of the "extremist" plays (1919–21) is that of the ambitious, driving, and all but heartless father. The extremists find their way out of the fog by clinging to an aggressive, domineering image of the self. But this image turns out to be a false one, a mask which covers no face at all. The face, the real self, has been sold for the crazy power and illusive wealth represented by the mask. There can be no doubt, after reading *Long Day's Journey into Night*, that regardless of what James O'Neill really was, to his son he represented this kind of pseudosolution to the search for self. He is the father of all O'Neill's proud, exploitive and grasping fathers—but self-deluded and pitiable, too, for Tyrone, in turn, was fashioned by *his* fathers, unable to escape the past which they created for

Tyrone, Sr., is the successful star actor of a romantic melodrama, as was the real James O'Neill. He has sacrificed wife and children to his need for secure wealth, denied him in his childhood. Obsessively, he invests his money in land, to the deprivation of his family. Here, of course are Ephraim, Keeney, and Bartlett. With some justice his family blame Tyrone for most of their afflictions—his wife's need for drugs, one son's alcoholism and the other's illness and insecurity. Not only his desire for money, but his stubborn ignorance and defensive pride in his Irish-Catholic origin, reenforcing his drive to outdo the Yankees, have been at the root of the family ills. The tragedy of Tyrone is that, like the other extremists, he has sold his soul for the illusion of success. He finally looks behind the mask when at the end of *Long Day's Journey* he confesses to Edmund:

> Yes, maybe life overdid the lesson for me, and made a dollar worth too much, . . . I've never admitted this to anyone before, lad, but tonight I'm so heartsick I feel at the end of everything, and what's the use of fake pride and pretense. That God-damned play I bought for a song and made such a great success in—a great money success—it ruined me with its promise of an easy fortune. I didn't want to do anything else, and by the time I woke up to the fact I'd become a slave to the damned thing and did try other plays, it was too late. . . . What the hell was it I

> wanted to buy, I wonder, that was worth—Well, no matter. It's
> a late day for regrets.
>
> (act 3)

Only the more sensitive of the extremists, like Tyrone, ever see the truth or realize that the real self has been lost. Indeed, among O'Neill's heroes, the sensitive ones alone are wholly alive, the sufferers and the creators. O'Neill took this positive view of sensitivity in the sequence of plays written between 1921 and 1927, when he believed most consciously and emphatically that the real order and justice of life lay in the tragic tension between opposites. His finders embrace this destiny and discover the answer to disunity in the unity of process, in the organic continuum in which opposition is the source of growth. In his own portrait of the artist as a young man in *Long Day's Journey*, O'Neill makes Edmund one of these tormented finders. In a long monologue addressed to his father, Edmund describes this stage of his development, when like his outcast namesake in *King Lear* he cries, "Thou nature, art my goddess!" If he cannot find a home with his family or with society, he can at least be absorbed into the processes of nature, especially those of the sea, where nature and the unconscious become symbolically one.

> I dissolved in the sea, became white sails and flying spray, became beauty and rhythm, became moonlight and the ship and the high dim-starred sky! I belonged, without past or future, within peace and unity and a wild joy, within something greater than my own life, or the life of Man, to Life itself! To God, if you want to put it that way. . . . Like a saint's vision of beatitude. Like the veil of things as they seem drawn back by an unseen hand.
>
> (act 3)

This was the vision of Juan, Kukachin, Jim, Abbie and Eben, Dion Anthony, and finally, Lazarus. But

> Then the hand lets the veil fall and you are alone, lost in the fog again, and you stumble on toward nowhere, for no good reason! . . . It was a great mistake, my being born a man, I would have been much more successful as a sea gull or a fish. As it is, I will always be a stranger who never feels at home, who does not really want and is not really wanted, who can never belong, who must always be a little in love with death!
>
> (act 3)

Edmund is ill with tuberculosis—as O'Neill was in 1912—and faces the possibility of death with a characteristic mixture of fear and longing. In addition, he learns with infuriated disgust that his father intends to economize on the cost of curing him by sending him to an inferior, state-supported sanitorium rather than to a private one. In the course of the play the father finally understands what he is doing and consents to send Edmund to a private hospital, where, indeed, O'Neill went. For all this apparent biographical accuracy of the portrait of the young O'Neill as Edmund, there is, as Philip Weissman points out at least one serious omission: O'Neill's marriage to Kathleen Jenkins in 1909 and his divorce from her in 1912, and the birth in 1910 of Eugene, Jr., whom O'Neill did not see until he was ten years old. O'Neill may have had any of several conscious reasons for suppressing this event in *Long Day's Journey*. Dr. Weissman suggests, however, that this omission amounted to an unconscious repression and rejection of the marriage itself, with all its overtones of O'Neill's inadequacy as a husband and father. Weissman explained the gap further in terms of O'Neill's identification with his mother:

> O'Neill shows himself, denying his path of love, marriage and paternity, as his mother denies hers in her utterances. His drinking and wanderings serve to make him forget his commitments to earthly life, as his mother's addiction and somnambulance rendered her unaware of her husband and children. And now it seems that his tuberculosis for which he has to go to a sanitorium, as his mother goes to one for her addiction, will again remove them from their earthly life and attachments.

In "dream, drunkenness, death," to use Engel's phrase, Edmund has succeeded in losing the self which tortured him with its ambivalence—toward itself and toward the conflicting father and mother images within it. In the "finders" period O'Neill saw, and demonstrated in his characters, the dualities which tore him apart. The only hope for integration lay, he knew, in his acceptance, if not reconciliation, of the dualities. But they could coexist only in the ecstatic visions of a transcendent oneness, visions which revealed themselves to be intellectualizations of real self-acceptance —theoretic, neurotic solutions to a neurotic struggle between the masks of the pride system. These may vanish for a while in the vision, but no real self is left to take their place—nothing but the mist, the fog, and through it the dismal horn of fate.

To this fate—the "true, fated reality" of *Mourning Becomes Electra*— O'Neill returned in his next group of plays, whose protagonists are called here "the trapped." The change in the plays was chiefly one of emphasis. The tension between opposites which the finders had considered a supporting framework of life now becomes a trap. The conflict of forces which the characters must attempt to reconcile or escape is that between the conscious mind and the unconscious—the modern equivalent of Fate. The protagonists' inevitable failure to control the unconscious mind ultimately makes them victims of destiny, not triumphant victors like their predecessors. Their struggle is no less heroic; in fact, it is more in the tradition of classic tragedy, and they approach more closely the dignity of the classic tragic hero than do the finders, for they *act* their "symbolical celebration of life," they do not see a vision of it or preach it.

Nina in *Strange Interlude* and Reuben in *Dynamo* spend their lives in an unwilled effort to escape the trap of self; so does Lavinia of *Mourning Becomes Electra*. The difference is that Lavinia almost does escape, until the death of Orin. Then she, too, is swallowed up by the family guilt; she turns on her heel and marches deliberately back into the self which alone can give her expiation. Her farewell words are, "I've got to punish myself. . . . It takes the Mannons to punish themselves for being born!"

And it took O'Neill to punish himself in writing *Long Day's Journey*. There he marches with Lavinia back to the only justice which can give him peace. His letter to his wife, published with the play, tells its own story. In it he thanks Mrs. O'Neill for the "love and tenderness which gave me the faith in love that enabled me to face my dead at last and write this play—write it with deep pity and understanding and forgiveness for ALL the four haunted Tyrones."

Long Day's Journey was penance, and in the penance itself lay redemption. The penitent no longer cries for another way out, for love and forgiveness through religious faith, as he did in *Days without End*. But the pattern of that former yearning can still be traced in the posthumous play. Just as in his early notes for *Days without End* O'Neill tried to avoid turning to Catholicism for the answer, so in *Long Day's Journey* the young Edmund rejects his father's dogmatic and meaningless adherence to Catholicism, while at the same time Edmund sees his mother's longing for faith, and feels that longing in himself. But as O'Neill showed clearly in this family epitaph, formal religion could never be a telling force in his life, except as it was identified with his mother; it offered no more reality as a way out of the trap of self than did her way out by morphine. The final curtain of *Long Day's Journey* falls on the most pathetic and terrifying scene in the entire canon. Mary has withdrawn into the dream world of a past when, as a convent schoolgirl, she still had faith in the Virgin.

I knew she heard my prayer and would always love me and see no harm ever came to me so long as I never lost my faith in her. (*She pauses and a look of growing uneasiness comes over her face. . . .*) That was in the winter of senior year. Then in the spring something happened to me. Yes, I remember. I fell in love with James Tyrone and was so happy for a time. (*She stares before her in a sad dream. Tyrone stirs in his chair. Edmund and Jamie remain motionless.*)

(act 4)

Tyrone stirs with the memory of old guilt which O'Neill portrayed not only in *Long Day's Journey*, but in the person of Hickey in *The Iceman Cometh*; Edmund and James are motionless, helpless with the paralysis of Larry in that play and of Jim Tyrone in *A Moon for the Misbegotten*. James, Sr.'s resemblance to Hickey emerges in act 3 of *Long Day's Journey*, when Mary reveals that in the early years of their marriage Tyrone habitually disappeared, only to be brought home dead drunk to his young wife, waiting in "that ugly hotel room." At Mary's accusation, her son Edmund "bursts out with a look of accusing hate at his father," who, "overwhelmed by shame which he tries to hide," pleads, "Mary! Can't you forget–?" and Mary answers, like Hickey's wife, "No, dear. But I forgive. I always forgive you. So don't look so guilty."

Long Day's Journey is most closely related to the "fatal balance" plays in the character of James, Jr., whose story is continued in *A Moon for the Misbegotten*, set ten years later. Both the parents are dead, but the family Furies are still pursuing Jim to his death. He is cursed by all his parents' guilt, besides his own, all their conflicting love and hate, their drives toward escape and self-destruction. *Long Day's Journey* includes this theme but adds another—his relationship to Edmund.

Out of childhood jealousy, and envy of the promise shown in Edmund, Jamie deliberately sets his worshiping younger brother an example of cynicism and dissipated self-destruction, in the guise of sophistication and romantic adventure. Tyrone, Sr., constantly warns Edmund to beware of Jamie's "sneering serpent's tongue," and Jamie at last drunkenly confesses:

Mama and Papa are right. I've been rotten bad influence. . . . Did it on purpose to make a bum of you. Or part of me did. A big part. That part that's been dead so long. That hates life. My putting you wise so you'd learn from my mistakes. Believed that myself at times, but it's a fake. . . . Never wanted you succeed and make me look even worse by comparison. Wanted you to fail. Always jealous of you. Mama's baby, Papa's pet! . . . And it was your being born that started Mama on dope. I know that's not your fault, but all the same, God damn you, I can't help hating your guts— ! . . . But don't get wrong idea, Kid. I love you more than I hate you. . . . Make up your mind you've got to tie a can to me —get me out of your life—think of me as dead—tell people, "I had a brother, but he's dead."

(act 3)

But the influence was so deeply rooted that, dead or alive, O'Neill's brother became a part of him, identified often with himself. In the plays the figure of the elder brother changes. As Andy, in *Beyond the Horizon*, he is to be admired, then pitied for the mistakes which are his downfall. In *The Great God Brown*, he is to be feared as the trusted older friend, who steals up behind the child, Dion, when in Dion's words, "I was drawing a picture in the sand he couldn't draw, and hit me on the head with a stick and kicked out the picture in the sand. It wasn't what he'd done that made me cry, but him! I had loved and trusted him and suddenly the good God was disproved in his person" (2.3).

Jim's face with its "Mephistophelean cast," which sometimes, when he smiles without sneering, reveals a "humorous, romantic irresponsible Irish charm," is a constant shadow in O'Neill's consciousness. Often it is one of his own tormenting masks; the other, that of the poetic boy. Jim was born in O'Neill's first plays, and did not quite die in his last. His fate was foreshadowed as early as the curtain scene of *Beyond the Horizon*, when, as Andrew, he tried to fight the hopeless apathy into which Ruth had withdrawn. In the last three plays Ruth's night closes in upon Jim and upon O'Neill himself.

In *Iceman*, *Moon*, and *Long Day's Journey*, O'Neill returned to his tragic conception of life as an endless struggle between opposite images of the self. Now, however, the conflict is not only hopeless, as it was for "the trapped," but worthless. Man is not even endowed with dignity by virtue of his struggle; he is a bare, forked animal, unredeemed by heroism, who spends his life trying to live up to a lie, trying to perpetuate an illusory conception of himself. All values are equal; neither the self nor its conception has any real existence or importance, and all we can ask of each other is pity and forgiveness. So ends the lifelong day that dawned with O'Neill's searchers in the fog, children of his mother, Mary Tyrone, proceeded with the mad extremists led by his father, James, soared to ecstatic noon with the young Edmund and the finders—before the afternoon fog settled upon the trapped victims of the family fate. Hope in religion and family love briefly shone through, in *Days without End* and *Ah, Wilderness!*, only to fade back into the fog where nothing remains except, in the words of Archibald MacLeish,

> To feel how swift, how secretly,
> The shadow of the night comes on.

Long Day's Journey into Night is a tragedy with four heroes. It is tragedy —not melodrama or "slice of life"—because each of its protagonists is partly responsible for his own destruction and partly a victim of the family fate. This, I think, is the chief distinction between tragedy as a genre and other plays in which the protagonist suffers a change of fortune from good to bad. Tragedy is the superior art form, because it presents the human being's true dilemma. In melodrama the assumption is that man is totally responsible for his actions and that there is a simple eye-for-an-eye justice in the universe which rules that he will be punished if he is wicked and rewarded if he is virtuous. In the naturalistic drama the assumption is the opposite one —that man is the victim of forces utterly beyond his control— his glands, society, disease.

The truth, I think, is somewhere in between, and the last turn of the screw for the tragic hero is his discovery that he has been struck down not alone by villainy (his own or others) or fate, but by his own mistakes, rooted in his own character. And his mistakes could be ours, for he is "a man like ourselves."

This is not to say that any tragedy is necessarily a better play than any other serious drama. Some of O'Neill's plays which follow most closely the theoretical requirements of tragedy were his greatest failures as literature and drama, even when they were good theatrical spectacle. For this failure, there seem to be two principal reasons. First, O'Neill sometimes tries too hard to convince us of our "ennobling identity" with the characters on the stage; and second, he often *explains* the "symbolical celebration of life" instead of dramatizing it. Both these defects arise from O'Neill's own tragic flaw, his neurosis.

The inert, paralyzed state of mind of the characters in the last three plays—a condition from which death alone can bring release—is one logical conclusion to be drawn from the philosophy that life is suspended between hopelessly divergent opposites. But the entire process of formulating such a theory springs not from logic, but from the necessity of a sick mind to fulfill its own needs. O'Neill called this drive the "sickness of today," and so it is. But then, it was the sickness also of the medieval monk, wrestling with his "dryness of spirit." Psychology and sociology have made us more aware today than ever before of the quiet desperation in which most men lead their lives, in an "other-directed" society where all goals are impositions from without. The tragic situation of modern man lies in the abdication of the real individual self from the position of authority and decision-making in favor of self-images drawn from society's expectations. O'Neill struck the right note for twentieth-century tragedy; Arthur Miller and Tennessee Williams have developed his theme.

The Theatre of Revolt

Robert Brustein

As some of the dust begins to settle over the controversial reputation of Eugene O'Neill, and our interest shifts from the man to art, it becomes increasingly clear that O'Neill will be primarily remembered for his last plays. The earlier ones are not all without value, though none is thoroughly satisfying. Some contain powerful scenes; some have interesting themes; and some are sustained by the sheer force of the author's will. Still, the bulk of O'Neill dramatic writings before *Ah, Wilderness!* are like the groping preparatory sketches of one who had to write badly in order to write well; and in comparison with the late O'Neill even intermittently effective dramas like *The Hairy Ape, All God's Chillun Got Wings*, and *Desire under the Elms* are riddled with fakery, incoherence, and clumsy experimental devices. No major dramatist, with the possible exception of Shaw, has written so many second-rate plays.

An important task of the O'Neill critic, therefore, is to account for the extraordinary disparity in style and quality between the earlier and later work; and one might well begin by exploring the external conditions in which O'Neill's talents began to bud. For if the playwright's early blossoms were sere, the cultural climate which helped to nurture them was (and is) peculiarly uncongenial to the development of a serious artist. O'Neill came to prominence in the second and third decades of the century, when America was just beginning to relinquish its philistinism in order to genuflect before the shrine of Culture. The American culture craze was

From *The Theatre of Revolt: An Approach to Modern Drama.* © 1964 by Robert Brustein. Little, Brown, 1964.

largely directed towards the outsides of the literature, which is to say towards the personality of the artist rather than the content of his art; and the novelists and poets inducted into this hollow ritual found themselves engaged in an activity more priestly than creative. O'Neill's role was especially hieratic, however, since he had the misfortune to be the first dramatist with serious aspirations to appear on the national scene. As George Jean Nathan noted, O'Neill "singlehanded waded through the dismal swamplands of American drama, bleak, squashy, and oozing sticky goo, and alone and singlehanded bore out the water lily that no American had found there before him." That the water lily sometimes resembled a cauliflower, Mr. Nathan was occasionally willing to concede. But to a large body of hungry critics and cultural consumers, who were indifferent to the quality of the product so long as it was Big, O'Neill was a homegrown dramatic champion to be enlisted not only against Ibsen, Strindberg, and Shaw, but against Aeschylus, Euripides, and Shakespeare as well.

In every superficial way, O'Neill certainly looked the role he was expected to fill. A dark, brooding figure with a strain of misfortune in his life, he combined the delicate constitution of a sensitive poet with the robust pugnacity of a barroom Achilles; and his youthful adventures as a seaman, gold prospector, and tramp had a rotogravure appeal to a nation already convinced by the Sunday supplements that an artist needed Vast Experience in order to write about Real Life. O'Neill, in addition, possessed the kind of aspiring mind which F. Scott Fitzgerald assigned to Jay Gatsby; he "sprang from his Platonic conception of himself." Afflicted with the American disease of gigantism, O'Neill developed ambitions which were not only large, they were monstrous; he was determined to be nothing if not a world-historical figure of fantastic proportion. Trying to compress within his own career the whole development of dramatic literature since the Greeks, he set himself to imitate the most ambitious writers who ever lived—and the more epic their scope, the more they stimulated his competitive instinct. The scope of his own intentions is suggested by the growing length of his plays and the presumptuousness of his public utterances. *Mourning Becomes Electra*, which took three days to perform, he called "an idea and a dramatic conception that has the possibilities of being the biggest thing modern drama has attempted—by far the biggest!" And his unfinished eleven-play "Big Grand Opus," as he called it, was designed to have "greater scope than any novel I know of . . . something in the style of *War and Peace*." At this point in his career, O'Neill, like his public, is attracted to the outsides of literature, and he wrestles with the reputation of another writer in order to boost his own. But to O'Neill's public, ambitions were almost indistinguishable from achievements; and the playwright was ranked with the world's greatest dramatists before he had had an opportunity to master his craft or sophisticate his art.

It was inevitable, therefore, that the next generation of critics—Francis Fergusson, Lionel Trilling, Eric Bentley—should harp on O'Neill's substantial failings as a thinker, artist, and Broadway hero. Subjected to closer scrutiny, the very qualities which had inspired so much enthusiasm in O'Neill's partisans now seemed the marks of a pretentious writer and a second-rate mind. Pushed about by this critical storm, the winds of literary fashion shifted, and O'Neill's reputation was blown out to sea. Although the playwright was awarded the Nobel prize in 1936, obscurity had already settled in upon him, and it deepened more and more until his death in 1953. During these dark years, ironically, O'Neill's real development began. Before, he had prided himself on having "the guts to shoot at something big and risk failure"; now, he had the guts not to bother himself about questions of success and failure at all. Maturing in silence, stimulated only by an obsessive urge to write and a profound artistic honesty, he commenced to create plays which were genuine masterpieces of the modern theatre. Most of these were not published or produced until after his death, some by the playwright's order. In proscribing *Long Day's Journey into Night*, O'Neill was trying to hide his family's secrets from the public eye; but O'Neill's desire to keep his works off the stage was undoubtedly influenced, too, by the hostile reception accorded to *The Iceman Cometh* and *A Moon for the Misbegotten*, the first of which failed on Broadway, the second, before even reaching New York. The public and the reviewers, having found new idols to worship (the Critic's prize the year of *The Iceman Cometh* went to a conventional social protest play by Arthur Miller called *All My Sons*), began to treat O'Neill with condescension—when they thought of him at all. And he was not to be seriously reconsidered until 1956, when a successful revival of *The Iceman Cometh* and the first Broadway production of *Long Day's Journey* brought him so much posthumous recognition that his inferior work was soon dragged out of storage for some more unthinking praise.

O'Neill's career, then, can be split into two distinct stages, which are separated not only by his changing position in the official culture, but by changes in style, subject matter, form, and posture as well. The first stage, beginning with the *S.S. Glencairn* plays (1913–16) and ending with *Days without End* (1932–33) is of historical rather than artistic interest: I shall discuss these plays [elsewhere] in a general way, as illustrations of O'Neill's early links with the theatre of revolt. The second stage is preceded by a transitional play, *Ah, Wilderness!* (1932), and contains *A Touch of the Poet*

(1935–42) the unfinished *More Stately Mansions* (1935–41), both from the cycle, *The Iceman Cometh* (1939), *Long Day's Journey into Night* (1939–41), and *A Moon for the Misbegotten* (1943). All of these works have artistic interest, but *The Iceman Cometh* and *Long Day's Journey* are, in my opinion, great works of art; these two I shall examine in some detail, as examples of the highly personal revolt which O'Neill pulled out of his own suffering. By contrasting the two stages in O'Neill's drama, I hope to illustrate O'Neill's development from a self-conscious and imitative pseudo-artist into a genuine tragic dramatist with a uniquely probing vision. . . .

This extraordinary play [*The Iceman Cometh*, discussed in a section of this essay not reprinted here] is a chronicle of O'Neill's own spiritual metamorphosis from a messianic into an existential rebel, the shallow yea-saying salvationist of the earlier plays having been transformed into a penetrating analyst of human motive rejecting even the pose of disillusionment. O'Neill's "denial of any other experience of faith in my plays" has left him alone, at last, with existence itself; and he has looked at it with a courage which only the greatest tragic dramatists have been able to muster. *The Iceman Cometh*, despite its prosaic language, recreates that existential groan which is heard in Shakespeare's tragedies and in the third choral poem of Sophocles's *Oedipus at Colonus*, as O'Neill makes reality bearable through the metaphysical consolations of art. O'Neill has rejected Hickey's brand of salvation as a way to human happiness, but truth has, nevertheless, become the cornerstone of his drama, truth combined with the compassionate understanding of Larry Slade. Expunging everything false and literary from his work, O'Neill has finally reconciled himself to being the man he really is.

This kind of reconciliation could only have come about through penetrating self-analysis; and it is inevitable, therefore, that the process of self-analysis itself should form the material of one of his plays: *Long Day's Journey into Night* (1939–41). Here, combining the retrospective techniques of Ibsen with the exorcistic attack of Strindberg, O'Neill compresses the psychological history of his family into the events of a single day, and the economy of the work, for all its length, is magnificent. Within this classical structure, where O'Neill even observes the unities, the play begins to approach a kind of formal perfection. Like most classical works, *Long Day's Journey* is set in the past—the summer of 1912, when O'Neill, then twenty-four, was stricken with tuberculosis, a disease which sent him to the sanatorium where he first decided to become a dramatist. And like most classical works, its impact derives less from physical action (the play has hardly any plot, and only the first act has any suspense) than from psychological revelation, as the characters dredge up their painful memories and half-considered thoughts. O'Neill's model is probably Ibsen's *Ghosts* (even Ibsen's title is singularly appropriate to the later play), because he employs that technique of exhumation which Ibsen borrowed from Sophocles—inching forward and moving backward simultaneously by means of a highly functional dialogue.

O'Neill, however, is not only the author of the play but also a character in it; like Strindberg, he has written "a poem of desperation," composed in rhythms of pain. The author's relation to his material is poignantly suggested in his dedication of the work to his wife, Carlotta, on the occasion of their twelfth anniversary: "I mean it as a tribute to your love and tenderness which gave me the faith in love that enabled me to face my dead at last and write this play—write it with deep pity and understanding and forgiveness for *all* the four haunted Tyrones." O'Neill includes himself in the general amnesty; he has certainly earned the right. The play, written as he tells us "in tears and blood," was composed in a cold sweat, sometimes fifteen hours at a stretch: O'Neill, like all his characters, is confronting his most harrowing memories, and putting his ghosts to rest in a memorial reenactment of their mutual suffering and responsibility.

Because his purpose is partially therapeutic, O'Neill has hardly fictionalized this autobiography at all. The O'Neills have become the Tyrones, his mother Ella is now called Mary, and Eugene takes on the name of his dead brother Edmund (the dead child is called Eugene), but his father and brother retain their own Christian names, and all the dramatic events (with a few minor changes) are true, including the story about the pigs of Tyrone's tenant farmer and the ice pond of the Standard Oil millionaire, an episode to be treated again in *A Moon for the Misbegotten*.

In view of this fidelity to fact, it is a wonder that O'Neill was able to write the play at all, but he is in astonishing control of his material—the work is a masterpiece. While *The Iceman Cometh* has fewer arid stretches and deeper implications, *Long Day's Journey* contains the finest writing O'Neill ever did—and the fourth act is among the most powerful scenes in all dramatic literature. O'Neill has created a personal play which bears on the condition of all mankind; a bourgeois family drama with universal implications. *Long Day's Journey* is a study of hereditary guilt which does not even make recourse to arbitrary metaphors, like Ibsen's use of disease in *Ghosts*. Edmund's consumption, unlike Oswald's syphilis, has a bacterial rather than a symbolic source. It is no longer necessary for O'Neill to invent a modern equivalent of Fate, for now he feels it working in his very bones. Thus, O'Neill's characters are suffering from spiritual and psychological ailments rather than biological and social ones (society, for O'Neill, hardly seems to exist), but they are just as deeply ravaged as Oswald and Mrs. Alving. O'Neill's achievement is all the more stunning when we remember that his previous efforts to write this kind of play were dreadfully bungled. In *Mourning Becomes Electra*, for example, the sins of the father are also visited on the sons, but this is illustrated through physical transformations—Orin begins to look like Ezra, Lavinia like Christine—a purely mechanical application of the theme. And the same sort of self-conscious contrivance is apparent in *Desire under the Elms*, where endless argumentation occurs over whether Eben is more like his "Maw" or his "Paw."

In *Long Day's Journey*, O'Neill has dismissed such superficial concerns to concentrate on the deeper implications of his theme: what is visited on the sons is a strain of blank misfortune. Here is a family living in a close symbiotic relationship, a single organism with four branches, where a twitch in one creates a spasm in another. O'Neill was beginning to explore this kind of relationship in *The Iceman Cometh*, where the derelicts aggravate each other's agony and hell is other people, but here he has worked out the nightmare of family relations with relentless precision. No individual character trait is revealed which does not have a bearing on the lives of the entire family; the play is nothing but the truth, but there is nothing irrelevant in the play. Thus, the two major characteristics which define James Tyrone, Sr.—his miserliness and his career as an actor—are directly related to the misery of his wife and children. Tyrone's niggardliness has caused Mary's addiction, because it was a cut-rate quack doctor who first introduced her to drugs; and Tyrone's inability to provide her with a proper home, because he was always on the road, has intensified her bitterness and sense of loss. The miser in Tyrone is also the source of Edmund's resentment, since Tyrone is preparing to send him to a State Farm for treatment instead of to a more expensive rest home. Edmund's tuberculosis, in turn, partially accounts for Mary's resumption of her habit, because she cannot face the fact of his bad health; and Edmund's birth caused the illness which eventually introduced his mother to drugs. Jamie is affected by the very existence of Edmund, since his brother's literary gifts fill him with envy and a sense of failure; and his mother's inability to shake her habit has made him lose faith in his own capacity for regeneration. Even the comic touches are structured along causal lines: Tyrone is too cheap to burn the lights in the parlor, so Edmund bangs his knee on a hatstand, and Jamie stumbles on the steps. Every action has a radiating effect, and characters interlock in the manner which evoked the anguished cry from Strindberg: "Earth, earth is hell. . . . in which I cannot move without injuring the happiness of others, in which others cannot remain happy without hurting me."

The family, in brief, is chained together by resentment, guilt, recrimination; yet, the chains that hold it are those of love as well as hate. Each makes the other suffer through some unwitting act, a breach of love or faith, and reproaches follow furiously in the wake of every revelation. But even at the moment that the truth is being blurted out, an apologetic retraction is being formed. Nobody really desires to hurt. Compassion and understanding alternate with anger and rancor. Even Jamie, who is "forever making sneering fun of somebody" and who calls his mother a "hophead," hates his own bitterness and mockery, and is filled with self-contempt. The four members of the family react to each other with bewildering ambivalence—exposing illusions and sustaining them, striking a blow and hating the hand that strikes. Every torment is self-inflicted, every angry word reverberating in the conscience of the speaker. It is as if the characters existed only to torture each other, while protecting each other, too, against their own resentful tongues.

There is a curse on the blighted house of the Tyrones, and the origin of the curse lies elsewhere, with existence itself. As Mary says, "None of us can help the things life has done to us." In tracing down the origin of this curse, O'Neill has returned to the year 1912; but as the play proceeds, he brings us even further into the past. Implicated in the misfortunes of the house are not only the two generations of Tyrones, but a previous generation as well; Edmund's attempted suicide, before the action begins, is linked to the suicide of Tyrone's father, and Edmund's consumption is the disease by which Mary's father died. Though O'Neill does not mention this, the tainted legacy reaches into the future, too: the playwright's elder son, Eugene Jr., is also to commit suicide, and his younger son, Shane, is to become, like his grandmother, a narcotics addict. The generations merge, and so does Time. "The past is the present, isn't it?" cries Mary. "It's the future too. We all try to lie out of that but life won't let us."

O'Neill, the probing artist, seeks in the past for the origination of guilt and blame; but his characters seek happiness and dreams. All four Tyrones share an intense hatred of the present and its morbid, inescapable reality. All four seek solace from the shocks of life in nostalgic memories, which they reach through different paths. For Mary, the key that turns the lock of the past is morphine. "It kills the pain. You go back until at last you are beyond its reach. Only the past when you were happy is real." The pain she speaks of is in her crippled hands, the constant reminder of her failed dream to be a concert pianist, but even more it is in her crippled, guilty soul. Mary has betrayed all her hopes and dreams. Even her marriage is a betrayal, since she longed to be a nun, wholly dedicated to her namesake, the Blessed Virgin; but her addiction betrays her religion, family, and home. She cannot pray; she is in a state of despair; and the accusations of her family only aggravate her guilt. Mary is subject to a number of illusions —among them, the belief that she married beneath her—but unlike the derelicts of *Iceman*, who dream of the future, she only dreams of the past. Throughout the action, she is trying to escape the pain of the present entirely; and at the end, with the aid of drugs, she has finally returned to the purity, innocence, and hope of her girlhood. Although the title of the play suggests a progress, therefore, the work moves always backwards. The long journey is a journey into the past.

O'Neill suggests this in many ways, partly through ambiguous images of light and dark, sun and mist. The play begins at 8:30 in the morning with a trace of fog in the air, and concludes sometime after midnight, with the house fogbound—the mood changing from sunny cheer over Mary's apparent recovery to gloomy despair over her new descent into hell. The nighttime scenes occur logically at the end of the day; but subjectively, the night precedes the day, for the play closes on a phantasmagoria of past time. Under the influence of Mary's drugs—and, to some extent, the alcohol of the men—time evaporates and hovers, and disappears: past, present, future become one. Mary drifts blissfully into illusions under cover of the night, which functions like a shroud against the harsh, daylight reality. And so does that fog that Mary loves: "It hides you from the world and the world from you," she says. "You feel that everything has changed, and nothing is what it seemed to be. No one can find or touch you any more." Her love for her husband and children neutralized by her terrible sense of guilt, Mary withdraws more and more into herself. And this, in turn, intensifies the unhappiness of the men: "The hardest thing to take," says Edmund, "is the blank wall she builds around herself. Or it's more like a bank of fog in which she hides and loses herself. . . . It's as if, in spite of loving us, she hated us."

Mary, however, is not alone among the "fog people"—the three men also have their reasons for withdrawing into night. Although less shrouded in illusion than Mary, each, nevertheless, haunts the past like a ghost, seeking consolation for a wasted life. For Tyrone, his youth was a period of artistic promise when he had the potential to be a great actor instead of a commercial hack; his favorite memory is of Booth's praising his Othello, words which he has written down and lost. For Jamie, who might have borne the Tyrone name "in honor and dignity, who showed such brilliant promise," the present is without possibility; he is now a hopeless ne'er-do-well, pursuing oblivion in drink and the arms of fat whores while mocking his own failure in bathetic, self-hating accents: "My name is Might-Have Been," he remarks, quoting from Rossetti, "I am also called No More, Too Late, Farewell." For Edmund, who is more like his mother than the others, night and fog are a refuge from the curse of living:

> The fog was where I wanted to be. . . . That's what I wanted— to be alone with myself in another world where truth is untrue and life can hide from itself. . . . It was like walking on the bottom of the sea. As if I had drowned long ago. As if I was a ghost belonging to the fog, and the fog was the ghost of the sea. It felt damned peaceful to be nothing more than a ghost within a ghost.

Reality, truth, and life plague him like a disease. Ashamed of being human, he finds existence itself detestable: "Who wants to see life as it is, if they can help it? It's the three Gorgons in one. You look in their faces and die. Or it's Pan. You see him and die—that is, inside you—and have to go on living as a ghost."

"We are such stuff as manure is made on, so let's drink up and forget it"—like Strindberg, who developed a similar excremental view of human-kind, the young Edmund has elected to withdraw from Time by whatever means available, and one of these is alcohol. Edmund, whose taste in poetry is usually execrable, finally quotes a good poet, Baudelaire, on the subject of drunkenness: "Be drunken, if you would not be martyred slaves of Time; be drunken continually! With wine, with poetry, or with virtue, as you will." And in order to avoid being enslaved by Time, Edmund contemplates other forms of drunkenness as well. In his fine fourth-act speech, he tells of his experiences at sea, when he discovered Nirvana for a moment, pulling out of Time and dissolving into the infinite:

> I belonged, without past or future, within peace and unity and a wild joy, within something greater than my own life, or the life of Man, to Life itself! To God, if you want to put it that way. . . . For a second you see—and seeing the secret, are the secret. For a second there is meaning! Then the hand lets the veil fall and you are alone, lost in the fog again, and you stumble on towards nowhere, for no good reason!

The ecstatic vision of wholeness is only momentary, and Edmund, who "would have been more successful as a sea-gull or a fish," must once again endure the melancholy fate of living in reality: "As it is, I will always be a stranger who never feels at home, who does not really want and is not really wanted, who can never belong, who must always be a little in love with death!" In love with death since death is the ultimate escape from Time, the total descent into night and fog.

There is a fifth Tyrone involved in the play—the older Eugene O'Neill. And although he has superimposed his later on his earlier self (Edmund, described as a socialist and atheist, has many religious-existential attitudes), the author and the character are really separable. Edmund wishes to deny Time, but O'Neill has elected to return to it once again—reliving the past and mingling with his ghosts—in order to find the secret and meaning of their suffering. For the playwright has discovered another escape besides alcohol, Nirvana, or death from the terrible chaos of life: the escape of art where chaos is ordered and the meaningless made meaningful. The play itself is an act of forgiveness and reconciliation, the artist's lifelong resentment disintegrated through complete understanding of the past and total self-honesty.

These qualities dominate the last act, which proceeds through a sequence of confessions and revelations to a harrowing climax. Structurally, the act consists of two long colloquies—the first between Tyrone and Edmund, the second between Edmund and Jamie—followed by a long soliloquy from Mary who, indeed, concludes every act. Tyrone's confession of failure as an actor finally makes him understandable to Edmund who thereupon forgives him all his faults; and Jamie's confession of his ambivalent feelings towards his brother, and his half-conscious desire to make him fail too, is the deepest psychological moment in the play. But the most honest moment of self-revelation occurs at the end of Edmund's speech, after he has tried to explain the origin of his bitterness and despair. Tyrone, as usual, finds his son's musings "morbid," but he has to admit that Edmund has "the makings of a poet." Edmund replies:

> The *makings* of a poet. No, I'm afraid I'm like the guy who is always panhandling for a smoke. He hasn't even got the makings. He's got only the habit. I couldn't touch what I tried to tell you just now. I just stammered. That's the best I'll ever do. . . . Well, it will be faithful realism, at least. Stammering is the native eloquence of us fog people.

In describing his own limitations as a dramatist, O'Neill here rises to real eloquence; speaking the truth has given him a tongue. Having accepted these limitations, and dedicated himself to a "faithful realism" seen through the lens of the "family kodak," he has turned into a dramatist of the very first rank.

Mary's last speech is the triumph of his new dramatic method, poetically evoking all the themes of the play; and it is marvelously prepared for. The men are drunk, sleepy, and exhausted after all the wrangling; the lights are very low; the night and fog very thick. Suddenly, a *coup de théâtre*. All the bulbs in the front parlor chandelier are illuminated, and the opening bars of a Chopin waltz are haltingly played, "as if an awkward schoolgirl were practising it for the first time." The men are shocked into consciousness as Mary enters, absentmindedly trailing her wedding dress. She is so completely in the past that even her features have been transfigured: "the uncanny thing is that her face now appears so youthful." What follows is a scene remarkably like Lady Macbeth's sleepwalking scene, or, as Jamie cruelly suggests, Ophelia's mad scene—an audaciously theatrical and, at the same time, profoundly moving expression from the depths of a tormented soul.

While the men look on in horror, Mary reenacts the dreams of her youth, oblivious of her surroundings; and her speeches sum up the utter hopelessness of the entire family. Shy and polite, like a young schoolgirl, astonished at her swollen hands and at the elderly gentleman who gently takes the wedding dress from her grasp, Mary is back in the convent, preparing to become a nun. She is looking for something, "something I need terribly," something that protected her from loneliness and fear: "I can't have lost it forever. I would die if I thought that. Because then there would be no hope." It is her life, and, even more, her faith. She has had a vision of the Blessed Virgin, who had "smiled and blessed me with her consent." But the Mother Superior has asked her to live like other girls before deciding to take her vows, and she reluctantly has agreed:

> I said, of course, I would do anything she suggested, but I knew it was simply a waste of time. After I left her, I felt all mixed up, so I went to the shrine and prayed to the Blessed Virgin and found peace again because I knew she heard my prayer and would always love me and see no harm ever came to me so long as I never lost my faith in her.

But the faith has turned yellow, like her wedding dress, and harm has indeed come. On the threshold of the later horror, Mary grows uneasy; then puts one foot over into the vacancy which is to come: "That was in the winter of senior year. Then in the springtime something happened to me. Yes, I remember. I fell in love with James Tyrone and was so happy for a time."

Her mournful speech, which concludes on the key word of the play, spans the years and breaks them, recapitulating all the blighted hopes, the

persistent illusions, the emotional ambivalence, and the sense of imprisonment in the fate of others that the family shares. It leaves the central character enveloped in fog, and the others encased in misery, the night deepening
around their shameful secrets. But it signalizes O'Neill's journey out of the
night and into the daylight—into a perception of his true role as a man and
an artist—exorcising his ghosts and "facing my dead at last."

In the plays that follow, O'Neill continues to work the vein he had
mined in *The Iceman Cometh* and *Long Day's Journey*: examining, through the
medium of a faithful realism, the people of the fog and their illusionary
lives. And in writing these plays, he stammers no more. In the lilting
speech of predominantly Irish-Catholic characters, O'Neill finally discovers
a language congenial to him, and he even begins to create a music very
much like Synge's, while his humor bubbles more and more to the surface.
Despite effective comic passages, however, O'Neill's plays remain dark. In
A Touch of the Poet, for example, he deals with a nineteenth-century Irish-
American tavernkeeper, Con Melody, who deludes himself that he is a
heroic Byronic aristocrat, proudly isolated from the Yankee merchants and
the democratic mob. Cold and imperious towards his wife but full of dash
and style, Melody undergoes a startling change when his illusions are exposed, groveling like a cunning and mean-spirited peasant. Poor but proud
before, he will now advance himself through any form of chicanery; but he
survives as a spiritually dead man, another of O'Neill's living corpses.

In *A Moon for the Misbegotten*, O'Neill follows Jamie O'Neill, the living
corpse of *Long Day's Journey*, into a later stage of his life, after the death of
his mother. Whiskey-logged and lacerated by self-hatred, he confesses to
an enormous but kindly girl (a virgin pretending to be promiscuous) how
he stayed with a whore on the train carrying his mother's corpse back East.
Sleeping all night on the ample bosom of this symbolic mother, like Jesus in
the Pietà, he earns from her the forgiveness and peace that the dead mother
can no longer provide.

These two works are minor masterpieces; *The Iceman Cometh* and
Long Day's Journey major ones. And in all four plays, O'Neill concentrates a
fierce, bullish power into fables of illusion and reality, shot through with
flashes of humor, but pervaded by a sense of melancholy over the condition
of being human. Like Strindberg, therefore, O'Neill develops from messianic rebellion into existential rebellion, thus demonstrating that beneath
his Nietzschean yea-saying and affirmation of life was a profound discontent with the very nature of existence. O'Neill's experiments with form,
his flirtations with various philosophies and religions, his attitudinizing and
fake poeticizing represent the means by which he tried to smother this

perception; but it would not be smothered, and when he finally found the courage to face it through realistic probes of his own past experience, he discovered the only artistic role that really fit him. In power and insight, O'Neill remains unsurpassed among American dramatists, and, of course, it is doubtful if, without him, there would have been an American drama at all. But it is for his last plays that he will be remembered—those extraordinary dramas of revolt which he pulled out of himself in pain and suffering, a sick and tired man in a shuttered room, unable to bear much light.

*L*ong Day's Journey into Night: Eugene O'Neill

Raymond Williams

When Eugene O'Neill died in 1953, he left three plays in manuscript, and among them *Long Day's Journey into Night*, dated 1940 on the manuscript but first produced in Stockholm in 1956. The play has a haunting effect: the reestablishment, as a living voice, of a dramatist whose main work had belonged to the 1920s and early 1930s; but also, in its power, the adding of a dimension, a necessary dimension, to all that earlier work. What came back into the theatre, in this posthumous play, was not only the voice of O'Neill, now especially intense and convincing. It was also the voice of that fully serious naturalism of the first epoch of modern drama: of Ibsen and of early Strindberg. It might have seemed like a ghost walking, but in all essential respects this was a powerful contemporary voice.

The sense of return, of the *revenant*, is of course overpowering, but as a direct dramatic experience. O'Neill spoke, in a note to his wife on the manuscript, of "the faith in love that enabled me to face my dead at last." It is the voice of late Ibsen, though not in imitation. The paradox of O'Neill's work, always, had been the strength of his realism, in a vernacular which created the modern American theatre, and his devices of distance, artifice, theatre in quite another sense. There is of course still power in *The Hairy Ape* and *Anna Christie*, in *Desire under the Elms*, *The Great God Brown*, *Strange Interlude* and *Emperor Jones*; but what I think is clear in O'Neill throughout, until these last plays, is a crisis of form which makes him a significant

From *Drama from Ibsen to Brecht*. © 1952 and 1968 by Raymond Williams. Oxford University Press, 1968.

figure. As in *Mourning Becomes Electra*, there is a sense of an intense experience just behind the play, just beyond what seemed the daring formal or theatrical experiment. Cast into what seemed, at the time, the new exploratory forms, the intensity in fact stiffened, became awkward: not gauche, which is on every count the wrong thing to say, but often falsely self-conscious, carrying out a literary act, surprising a theatre. There were many dramatists who used these new forms in a direct relation to a structure of feeling which supported them. The paradox of O'Neill was a sense of projection when all the substantial feeling was direct; of formalism, when all the driving emotion was in a different, more immediate voice. My own sense, when I came to *Long Day's Journey into Night*, was of release and discovery: that hidden drama, of the earlier work, was at last directly written, and the power flowed, now at last in its authentic channels.

Many voices are heard in this play which was new in the mid-1950s: the Ibsen reckoning, the calling-to-account of a family; the Strindberg intensity, as direct confrontation breaks through the prepared defences; and also, unexpectedly, the experience of that Irish drama, now set in another country, where the persistent tension is between an intense reality and a way of talking, of talking well, to avoid it. It is an autobiographical play: that is one way of describing it. O'Neill faces his dead—the Tyrone family, the O'Neills. But though the correspondences are obvious, it is not the autobiography that makes the play important, it is that what is commonly faced in displaced forms is now faced directly, not as a documentary record but as an imaginative summoning. What comes out elsewhere as a conclusion—the sense of deadlock, of isolation, of insubstantial and destructive relationships—comes out here as a process: not those static forms dramatized, as a single act, but their complex formation pressed deeply into a consciousness which is the controlling convention. Much of the drama of the last forty years has been the last act, the last scene, of an earlier phase, presented, with increasing sophistication, as a whole history. Men are lost, frustrated, isolated, in a world of illusion and self-deception, a world they have distorted and is now only distorted: that condition, which is always a consequence, has become an assumption, is where the new conventions start. O'Neill, who had made this assumption as powerfully and as conventionally as anyone else, now goes back behind it, and shows the experience as active. The action takes place in one day—the day's experience of the title. But the convention is not of a static situation, or of the last stage of deadlock. It is a calling to account, a facing of facts, inside this family; but not to prove anything, by some retrospective formula. It is a searching of the past, to define the present, but because all the family are speaking, it is not one selected past, but a range of past experiences now relived and altering the present: not memory but recreation, with the possibilities as well as the failures acted out.

This essential and liberating strength can be seen most clearly in the writing of the mother: now drugging herself with morphine against the pain of present and past. The pain and the drugging are directly powerful, but they release—as in different ways in the others—at once the intense confession, the necessary involvement with the pain of what the family has become, and the detachment from it: the ability to find both the truth and the fantasy of the past. Under the drug she is "detached," but it is a detachment in active presence, and this is the necessary dramatic means: that she can be the girl before her marriage but also, from her pain now as a wife and mother, the false idea of that girl—an involuntary, painful self-deception which has fed into the long destruction. Her husband, similarly, exists in his several possibilities and self-accounts: coming in poverty from Ireland and still buying land—irrelevant land—against the fear of dying in the poorhouse, in what is at once a substantial experience and a practised excuse; or as the actor, the man who can play a role—at once his gift, from which they live, and his power to deceive himself and others, in a continual shifting uncertainty. Each mode of the parents appears, disappears, comes back to be seen differently: this is the real haunting, the live haunting, of the many possibilities out of which a life is made and through which it can be seen: not separate possibilities, but interacting within each person, and crucially, between them, where the weaknesses interlock. The two sons, Jamie and Edmund, can be taken as contrasting characters, and indeed have this immediate substance; but they are also two living possibilities, of response, shaping and self-shaping to that parental relationship and, just as much, those shifting parental identities. There is the hard cynicism, or the lonely walking in the fog: neither able to realize a self: not mature, or not born, in this unfinished, unresolved parenthood.

In a later dramatic form, the roles would be separated, would be separately played, as conditions. What is replayed here, in the rush of the present, is the range of modes, in a still active process. It is defined in different ways: through the idea of the theatre, which has made and destroyed this family—so that when Mary comes in, drugged and in pain, in the last scene at midnight, both playing and being the hunted, remembering, day-dreaming girl, Jamie can say "the Mad Scene. Enter Ophelia!," and it is both true and false, about the scene and about her. Again, an element of Tyrone's deception is not only his acting manner—which he briskly resumes after the intervals of pain—but his willed Irish charm, a false consciousness, which can yet be contrasted with the rejection of Ireland, the rejection of the father, in Jamie —

> TYRONE. Keep your dirty tongue off Ireland. You're a fine one to
> sneer with the map of it on your face.
> JAMIE. Not after I wash my face. (*Then before his father can react to
> this insult to the Old Sod.*)

—and with the false consciousness of the cynicism of the new country, as in Edmund's parody:

> They never come back! Everything is in the bag! It's all a
> frame-up. We're all fall guys and suckers and we can't beat the
> game!

Each way of speaking is at once the truth of their experience and a way of avoiding the truth, in the conventional patter of one or other dialect.

What is said under drink or drug, or in anger and then in apology, or then soberly and honestly, is made part of the range: the interaction, of all the ways of speaking, is the dramatic truth. The true poetry and the false poetry, the feeling, the pretended feeling, the lie and the white lie, the substance and the performance: this, essentially, is the medium. It is bound to be uneven, but in scenes like that between Tyrone and Edmund at the beginning of the fourth act, which yet does not stand out but is an intensification of the continuing action, it has a power which reminds us what serious naturalism—the passion for truth, the relentless directness—was and is, as a dramatic movement. What the play relives, in its substance, is not only the history of a family, but of a literature. It is the long crisis of relationships, in a family and in a society, now again enacted directly, in and through a disintegration, while at the edges of this consciousness the forms of a late phase, of the consciousness of midnight after the long day's journey and pain, stand burning and ready: as if I had drowned long ago.

Through the Fog into the Monologue

Timo Tiusanen

In *Long Day's Journey into Night* O'Neill's reliance on the expressive power of his dialogue is still greater than in *The Iceman Cometh*. He has only five characters in his cast; there is no chorus, nor are there any changes in the setting; there is a most effective return to the repetitive sound effect. In spite of these dissimilarities the dynamics of these two plays work in a similar manner. Instead of transferring from one group of characters to another, O'Neill now goes from one theme to another. There is more variety of theme, less of character; all the four Tyrones stand out as fully individualized human beings, bound together by a common fate, by an in-escapable love-hate relationship. This tragedy has four protagonists. When working his way toward the final revelations, toward four magnificent modified monologues, O'Neill employed in his dialogue several solutions we know from *The Iceman Cometh*.

There are, first of all, the masks. Mary Tyrone has two masks in act 1, those of relaxed self-confidence and of nervousness. She is back at home after a cure in a sanatorium for drug addicts; the three Tyrone men have confidence in her ability to resist the temptation this time. Her gradual return to the old habit is the decisive change in the family situation during this long day's journey. It releases unexpected reactions in the others, in the famous actor James Tyrone, in his thirty-three-year-old actor son Jamie, a failure and an alcoholic, and in Edmund, a journalist ten years younger than his brother who is about to be sent to a tuberculosis sanatorium.

In act 1 there is still hope: the inner struggle is still going on in Mary.

From *O'Neill's Scenic Images*. © 1968 by Timo Tiusanen. Princeton University Press, 1968.

Hence the masks, given in the initial description of Mary and in the stage directions between and within the speeches: "What strikes one immediately is her extreme nervousness. Her hands are never still." Another fixing point for this mask is her hair: "(*She stops abruptly, catching Jamie's eyes regarding her with an uneasy, probing look. Her smile vanishes and her manner becomes self-conscious*) Why are you staring, Jamie? (*Her hands flutter up to her hair*)." The mask is made visible through these means, and there is interaction with changes in the tone of voice, with facial expressions, with the gestures and groupings.

The opening act closes with a pantomime by Mary. She makes the apprehensive men leave her alone, and the tension between her two roles is shown: "Her first reaction is one of relief. She appears to relax. . . . But suddenly she grows terribly tense again. Her eyes open and she strains forward, seized by a fit of nervous panic. She begins a desperate battle with herself. Her long fingers, warped and knotted by rheumatism, drum on the arms of the chair, driven by an insistent life of their own, without her consent."

The battle is lost. In the following acts Mary progresses deeper and deeper into the secluded world of a drug addict, swinging all the time between two roles, wearing alternately two masks. When she has her defenses up, no petitions from the others, no events on the stage, can reach her. She is as strangely detached as Deborah. And when she has not yet totally escaped, she feels guilty—of her irrational flight, of the death of one of her sons, called Eugene in the play, of Edmund having been born at all, of life in general. She may confess her concern for Edmund or her fear of consumption, she may speak of her own guilt—only to turn abruptly away again: "Then, catching herself, with an instant change to stubborn denial." It is foolish to worry; it is reassuring to cling to the pipe dream that Edmund has only a bad summer cold.

The further Mary recedes from the living room of the Tyrones, the clearer it becomes that her two roles are played behind the masks of her two different ages. "Her most appealing quality is the simple, unaffected charm of a shy convent-girl youthfulness she has never lost—an innate unworldly innocence." When she has escaped, when she wears the mask of detachment, she lives in her convent days again, far from James Tyrone and the shabby hotel rooms that have been her surroundings throughout her married life. This movement in the dimension of time resembles the dynamics in *More Stately Mansions* and *The Iceman Cometh*: Mary is a "one-time" convent girl. The masks, written into the stage directions, are given three different functions in the case of Mary Tyrone; they show the conflict between temptation and resistance, between her drugged and normal states, and between her adolescence and old age.

Mary is the best example of the application made of the masks in *Long Day's Journey into Night*, yet she is not the only one. The continuous vacillation between attachment and repulsion has been observed by several critics. In fact, each of the characters wears two masks in his relations to the other members of the family: those of love and hatred. The play is a chain of small circles, all touching the areas of mutual sympathy and antagonism, all obeying the mechanics of defenses, accusations, and counter-accusations. On the stage, the circles are drawn by the actors: their positions, gestures, vocal and facial expressions.

Temporary harmonies are possible, even between Tyrone and Jamie, two archenemies: "His son looks at him, for the first time with an understanding sympathy. It is as if suddenly a deep bond of common feeling existed between them in which their antagonisms could be forgotten." Yet in the next moment the pendulum swings toward bitter enmity; another circle is started. A primary vehicle for this incessant movement, in addition to the sudden, paradoxical change of masks, is the clipped quality of the dialogue. When Hickey was coming close to dangerous areas, to the mine fields of *The Iceman Cometh*, he interrupted his sentences, giving his listeners only a hint, letting only an uneasy suspicion form in their minds. It is so also in *Long Day's Journey into Night*.

We might speak of five different uses made of the interrupted sentences. Three of them are closely associated with the total dynamics of the play. (1) It is certainly not O'Neill's invention that the adversaries interrupt one another in emotionally tense scenes out of mere excitement; there are such cases in *Long Day's Journey*. (2) Especially in act 1 the Tyrones guard one another, preventing the speakers from approaching dangerous subjects of discussion—Edmund's illness, or Mary's newly aroused inclination, revealed by her movements the previous night. It is a family taboo even to suspect that Mary is not completely healed—and another that Edmund might be in real danger. Mary has barely hinted at her feeling that the men are keeping an eye on her when Edmund interrupts, "too vehemently": "I didn't think anything!" Or, Jamie has hardly interpreted a remark by Tyrone as an indication that the father is thinking of Edmund's death when he is checked by Tyrone, in a "guiltily explosive" speech.

(3) They are checked not only by one another but also by themselves. Examples of sentences interrupted by the speaker himself are numerous: the Tyrones often stop themselves right on the threshold of a terrible accusation or self-accusation. They need another drink or shot in the arm to

come out with the truth—as they finally do. Before they reach the stage of
modified monologues, they exercise introspection by leaving something
unsaid. "Please stop staring!" Mary exclaims. "One would think you were
accusing me—" of having taken morphine again, she is about to say, but
does not dare. Both this and the second usage have two functions: they add
to the tension of the play by creating secrets, and they leave an impression
that all of the characters know what is about to be revealed. This is not the
first time these circles are run through. They are parts of an incessant
discussion, parts of a relentless family fate, realized from year to year, from
day to day—and into night.

(4) A modification of this, not as dynamic, is the interruption as a
result of an overpowering feeling. There is nothing more to be added by
the speaker; the sentence is complete in its context, even if deficient in its
form. Tyrone speaks "shakenly" to Mary after one of her outpourings of
accusations against doctors, in spite of Edmund's presence and the delicacy
of the theme of death: "Yes, Mary, it's no time—"

(5) The last usage, again closely bound to the total dynamics, occurs
when one of the four interrupts a speaker, not so much because these two
were getting into an argument, as to give a helping hand to a third. "James,
do be quiet," Mary says to her husband who is reproaching Jamie. As in
More Stately Mansions there is no end of new frontiers being formed. The
boys react against Tyrone, the parents against their sons, all the men against
Mary; the mother defends her sons, each of them at different times. The
Iceman Cometh, with its massive dynamics, operated with a few emphatic
frontiers: the chorus for or against Hickey. Long Day's Journey into Night,
with its fewer characters, is a more fluid and labile play.

If we start looking for the roots of this kind of dialogue, it is possible
to go back as far as to the first fluctuating monologues in O'Neill. The
small circles drawn by Yank in The Hairy Ape in his efforts to overcome the
difficulties of communication have an affinity with the way the Tyrones
proceed. The circles are now drawn by several characters in their attempts
to understand. The last act of Welded, with its precarious harmony and
violent accusations, Strange Interlude, with its vacillation, and all of the mask
plays were important later developments. Essentially, this kind of dialogue
has dramatic rather than literary merits: it speaks not with striking verbal
images, but with its incessant movement. It has hardly been fully analyzed
or appreciated by the literary critics of drama.

It is an abstraction to say that the small circles in Long Day's Journey
into Night are formed by alternating love and hatred. The concrete elements
in a play are its themes: the circles are built out of bits of discussion, mostly
reminiscences. Instead of groups of characters, this play has groups of

speeches, each around a theme. The topics discussed include Mary's hatred of doctors, her convent days, her intolerable life in shabby hotels; Tyrone's stinginess, his hard childhood, his drinking habits; Jamie's failure, in all its varied aspects; Edmund's illness, his rebellious opinions on politics and literature, his experiences on the sea. None of these themes is given a conclusive treatment in the first three acts of the play: again, O'Neill is a careful builder of drama.

One theme is taken up and developed to an emotional climax, then there is a standstill until a new theme is picked up, to be treated in a similar way. This is a picture of O'Neill's total development, too: he picked up a certain scenic means of expression, developed it (often to an overuse), and then began working with another. Near the end of his career, he drew his means of expression together—as he did the themes of *Long Day's Journey*.

Even if the emphasis is on the dialogue, it is necessary to pay attention to the interaction of several scenic means of expression. The autobiographical character of the setting is of lesser interest to us than its functional aspects. One of the bookshelves may include most of the books young O'Neill read and admired; this is not, however, of great significance because their names and authors can hardly be made visible to the audience. The relation between Mary and the setting is, on the other hand, interesting: the house is inescapable to her, more so than to the others. We never see Mary leave the house; we know that when she goes out it is only to fetch more morphine. As a contrast, the departures of the men are demonstrated on the stage. Tyrone and Jamie go out to cut the hedge; Edmund takes a walk in the fog, escaping into his poetic vision; all three go downtown, have company, and come home drunk. They do come home—to carry the burden of their family fate.

Mary is deserted by the men: this is the impression conveyed by leaving her alone on the stage at the end of two scenes. Act 1 is closed with Mary's pantomime, quoted above. She is left even more emphatically alone at the close of act 2, scene 2, when Edmund leaves her in the living room, Tyrone and Jamie shout their "Goodbye, Mary" and "Goodbye, Mama" from the hall. She sighs of relief—only to go to the other extreme and give her curtain line: "Then Mother of God, why do I feel so lonely?" Whether to call this desertion symbolic or not is a pure conjecture; one might say that it is both completely realistic and deeply symbolic, at the same time. In fact, this is the way all scenic means of expression are employed in *Long Day's Journey into Night*: they have a multiple motivation, both realistic and symbolic.

All the outer world means to Mary is a place from which she can obtain drugs. James is the only one of the four who has contacts with the "respectable" people in the town: he can go on talking with them, even forgetting his family and the waiting meal in doing so. The specific place of action, between back and front parlors, is interpreted by Doris V. Falk: "The family 'lives' in that mid-region between the bright formality of the exterior front parlor—the mask—and the little-known dark of the rear-room." In addition to these symbolic overtones belonging to the setting as a whole, there is a significance attached to the rooms upstairs, where Mary is known or suspected to be drugging herself. Her character is firmly estab-lished in the first three acts, where she leaves the stage only to go into the two parlors and through the front parlor upstairs—so firmly established, in fact, that it is more suggestive to keep her off-stage through most of act 4. All that reminds us of her are references in the dialogue and the noise of her steps. Mary lives in the imagination of the audience—to come and make her shocking entrance at the end of the play.

There is an interaction between the setting, the foghorn, and Mary's modified monologue in act 3, in a scenic image that might be called a preliminary synthesis of Mary's role. She is again alone, right in the focus of interest; she has reached the stage of frankly confessional monologues earlier than the men; and then the foghorn comes, with its gloomy message of hopelessness. She has used Cathleen, the "second girl," as an excuse for her modified monologue, indicating how little choice she has in her search for human contacts. Now she is without company and relaxes, her fingers calm. Even the pause is recorded, as elsewhere in the play: "It is growing dark in the room. There is a pause of dead quiet. Then from the world outside comes the melancholy moan of the foghorn, followed by a chorus of bells, muffled by the fog, from the anchored craft in the harbor. Mary's face gives no sign she has heard, but her hands jerk and the fingers auto-matically play for a moment on the air. . . . She suddenly loses all the girlish quality and is an aging, cynically sad, embittered woman." Mary's shift from one role to another is given an emphatic treatment here by using the movements of her fingers and reminding us, once again, of one of her dreams: to become a concert pianist. In her monologue she expresses her disillusionment: not even the Blessed Virgin, whose consolation is her dearest pipe dream, cares to help a dope fiend. She has just decided to go and get some more morphine when the men come in, to end the scenic image, to relieve her from the joy and burden of loneliness, and to start the circular movement again.

The presence of the fog is conveyed to the audience through the foghorn and through references in the dialogue. Mary's attitude is typically ambivalent: the fog is both a disguise from the world and a symbol of her guilty escape. "It hides you from the world and the world from you," she explains to Cathleen. "You feel that everything has changed, and nothing is what it seemed to be. No one can find or touch you any more. . . . It's the foghorn I hate. It won't let you alone. It keeps reminding you, and warning you, and calling you back." Edmund has experienced the same fascination of escape during his walk in the fog: "Everything looked and sounded unreal. Nothing was what it is. That's what I wanted—to be alone with myself in another world where truth is untrue and life can hide from itself. . . . Who wants to see life as it is, if they can help it?" Yet Edmund comes back from the fog to describe his experience, to give it a verbal form, to turn it into art.

O'Neill specifies the use of the foghorn, with its connotations of fascination and dread, of fate and unreality, at three phases during the play. One of them is discussed above; one is an introductory usage at the beginning of act 3; the third will be discussed in this paragraph. Elsewhere, the foghorn is utilized as a kind of repetitive sound coulisse, to be resorted to according to the judgment of the stage director. In a scene between Mary and Edmund we have a beautiful example of O'Neill's sense of drama, in his transference from human expression into the foghorn. Edmund has voiced his bitterest accusation ("It's pretty hard to take at times, having a dope fiend for a mother!"), and immediately asks for forgiveness after seeing his mother's reaction—all life seems "to drain from her face, leaving it with the appearance of a plaster cast." There is a standstill, the emotion cannot be developed further; and this is where the foghorn is employed: "(*There is a pause in which the foghorn and the ships' bells are heard.*) MARY (*goes slowly to the windows at right like an automaton—looking out, a blank far-off quality in her voice*). Just listen to that awful foghorn. And the bells. Why is it fog makes everything sound so sad and lost, I wonder?" Another familiar scenic unit employed is the automaton effect, also met occasionally in *Long Day's Journey into Night*. As to this scenic image as a whole, we might speak of the old principle of "*pars pro toto*": O'Neill needed a sense of the total tragedy between mother and son, and evoked it by giving a concrete part of it— the noise of the foghorn.

The theme of the fog is given even a comic treatment in Jamie's homecoming. "The fron [sic] steps tried to trample on me," he complains in the beginning of his drunken and grotesquely comic appearance. "Took advantage of fog to waylay me. Ought to be a lighthouse out there." It is worth emphasizing that *Long Day's Journey into Night* is not void of comedy. One of the functions of Cathleen is to provide comic relief. She also plays confidante to Mary and has a choral function: "He's a fine gentleman," she says of Tyrone, "and you're a lucky woman." This is how the Tyrones must look in the eyes of outsiders; yet the opinion has an ironical effect in its context. So has her innocent remark somewhat earlier in the scene: "You've taken some of the medicine? It made you act funny, Ma'am." One of the excuses, here, as well as in *The Iceman Cometh*, is an unconvincing effort to be jocular—afterwards. Insults are "only teasing" or "only kidding."

Tyrone and Edmund begin to play cards early in act 4. But the compulsions to confess, to find sympathy, are stronger than the merely mechanical act of handling the cards. Tyrone begins to speak about the play he bought, and how he guaranteed his economic success and artistic failure with it: no one wanted to see him in any other role. Then he "glances vaguely at his cards" and asks: "My play, isn't it?" The intention is bitterly ironic: this is what is left of Tyrone's play, of his life—a handful of cards.

Stage action and groupings also interact with dialogue elsewhere. When Mary has taken her first dose of drug, everyone avoids looking at her. She herself goes behind Edmund, the most innocent and least suspicious of her men, to save him from the observation as long as possible. Two situations are repeated with variation, to show how Mary's position is changed by her fall. Tyrone, the closest person to her, enters together with her in act 1—and follows behind her in act 2, scene 2, in a similar entrance after a meal. He keeps beside Mary in their exit at the end of act 2, scene 1—and remains on the stage in act 3 after her exit "as if not knowing what to do. He is a sad, bewildered, broken old man. He walks wearily off." These changes occur in emphatic phases of the play; they are important indications of development in the relations between the characters. So is the scattered grouping at the beginning of act 2, scene 2. Tyrone and Jamie look out of the door and the window; Edmund sits so that he does not have to watch his mother. The family is falling apart.

A special feature in *Long Day's Journey into Night* is its plentiful quotations, most of which appear in act 4. They prepare the way for the confessions, they accentuate the tragic feeling created by the modified monologues. Leech is worried about O'Neill's taste when choosing the poems: "it appears they are quoted *con amore*, with the implication that they represent what poetry exclusively is" [Clifford Leech, *Eugene O'Neill* (1963)]. On the other hand, they are quoted both seriously and parodically. O'Neill is on his guard against sentimentality in this late play: before he reaches pathos, he turns around by using a sudden ironic twist. And there is no doubt that the quotations fulfill their basic function, described by Sigvard Mårtensson: they make it possible for the playwright to "express the elevated emotion, the strong tension otherwise not easily articulated by the realistic dialogue. The technique is employed with distinction and never breaks the frame" [*Eugene O'Neill's dramatik*]. It is quite natural to quote poetry in a family of two actors and a would-be author.

The central problem of guilt is touched on once by employing a Shakespearean quotation. "The fault, dear Brutus, is not in our stars, but in ourselves that we are underlings," James Tyrone sighs—not, however, recognizing his own fault. His quotations are ridiculed by his sons; as Raleigh has remarked, in O'Neill's last plays we "are asked to take nothing on faith." Tyrone's confidential disclosure of his failure is accepted as truth by Edmund and by the audience; yet its impact is lessened by the sneering Jamie a few minutes later: "He's been putting on the old sob act for you, eh?" And the ultimate question of guilt is left unsolved in this relativistic play: "Nothing is to blame except everybody." Fate, fog, life itself, all of us may be guilty—yet finding a scapegoat does not change at all our unredeemable situation.

Act 4 in *Long Day's Journey into Night* is magnificent; and the quotations help to make it so. Each of the four Tyrones is driven to his final confession in a modified monologue. Everything said or done in the play contributes to these revelation scenes, following one another in a series of scenic images. The first of these is analyzed [elsewhere]. Tyrone speaks of the ambitions of a young Shakespearean actor; and we realize, as Waith has acutely observed, "that his longing for his youth is no less poignant than his wife's." If ever the life of a human being has been weighed on the stage, in a manner both honest and warm, if ever deep tragedy is in the next moment followed by tragicomedy, this is the case [Eugene M. Waith, "Eugene O'Neill: An Exercise in Unmasking," *Educational Theatre Journal* 13 (October 1961): 182–91].

Edmund describes his experience of freedom and belonging on the sea. The passage is written in the same vein as the vision of Stephen Daedalus at the end of *A Portrait of the Artist as a Young Man*. "For a second you see—and seeing the secret, are the secret. For a second there is meaning!" —is not this what so many creative artists have experienced? The epiphany is presented as momentary, it is a part of a tragedy that certainly does not sing in rapture for the ecstasy of living; and it is followed, as many of Edmund's and Jamie's speeches are, by a self-ironic afterthought. "It was a great mistake," Edmund grins wryly, "my being born a man, I would have been much more successful as a sea gull or a fish." And he agrees with his father that he has perhaps only the makings of a poet: "I just stammered. That's the best I'll ever do. I mean, if I live. Well, it will be faithful realism, at least. Stammering is the native eloquence of us fog people."

This is only the second climax in the act: Jamie is still to be revealed, and the final synthesis of the family situation is still to be achieved by letting Mary join the others. So is a focusing synthesis of several scenic means of expression to come. Behind the mask of the brother and best friend who has "put Edmund wise" on women and the world in general there has been jealousy and resentment in Jamie: he hates and loves his brother—and his mother. His "love" meeting with Fat Violet in the town brothel is a grotesque revenge on Mary; he brought Violet upstairs—where Mary is in the Tyrone house. When remembering Mary's first fall, he identifies his mother with the whores: "Christ, I'd never dreamed before that any women but whores took dope!" Jamie is partly dead—he is destructive and poisonous—while Edmund feels that he belongs to Life itself. This time there is a contrast, not an equation, as between Mary and Tyrone: Edmund is called by Waith a "creator." Yet there is also love, of a helpless and moving kind, in Jamie: "Greater love hath no man than this, that he saveth his brother from himself."

The long day's journey into four monologues is completed, and everything is revealed, when Mary comes down and plays the piano "with a forgetful, stiff-fingered groping, as if an awkward schoolgirl were practicing . . . for the first time." Then she enters the final scenic image in the play, likewise described [elsewhere]. It looks for a while as if Edmund may break through her defenses; but only for a while. She soon returns into her fog, listens but does not hear Jamie quoting Swinburne (perfectly appropriately in this context), and says her curtain line from far away in her past.

According to certain formulas of critical thought, *Long Day's Journey into Night* should be a poor play. It is "undoubtedly too long—one long scene seems almost irrelevant; there is too much quoting of classic poetry; and the deliberate formlessness of it all is enervating. Still, it is a dramatic achievement of the first order," "a masterpiece." A euphemistic way of putting it is to say that the play is great "in spite of"—and then let the merits remain largely unanalyzed.

If a play is a masterpiece "in spite of" several critical presuppositions, it is high time to start asking whether there is anything wrong—with the presuppositions. If we have not given up the hope of finding rational explanations to art, we should be busy looking for reasons *why Long Day's Journey into Night* is a masterpiece—instead of weighing down the other end of the scale with our inapplicable criteria. One thing is certain: emotional power does not come through on the stage without some kind of technique; only physical power might. And *Long Day's Journey into Night* does not shout; it speaks through its form.

Admitting that the play is void of outer action, there is good reason to emphasize that it is full of inner action. It is within the speeches that a major part of the drama is acted; it is within the utterances that the masks are changed. O'Neill let himself be bound by the tradition of realism because he knew that he could utilize the amount of freedom granted to him by the shortish chain of this style. He was convinced of his ability to dance in these chains. He knew that he could write in a style infiltrated by the results of his experimental period; he knew how to achieve porousness by making every detail both realistic and symbolic. "His contrapuntal arrangement of events that are seen in the theatre and reported events, which become real in the theatre of the mind only, makes his realism a free and spacious style," Stamm writes, recognizing clearly an important aspect of O'Neill's dynamic realism. Yet the reminiscent speeches of *Long Day's Journey into Night* would be static if O'Neill had not employed his small circles, drawn to touch love and hatred, sympathy and antagonism, guilt and accusations. O'Neill does not only move backwards in time, he also makes the past present. The past is an actual phenomenon, not asking but demanding reactions from the agonized characters. The wild fluctuation in the mind of Caligula or Ponce de Leon was attached only to the stage situation; now O'Neill has also the rich orchestra of human memories to play with.

"The past is the present, isn't it? It's the future, too. We all try to lie out of that but life won't let us," Mary complains in one of her most lucid moments. If the first sentence could be taken as the motto for O'Neill's technique, the second reveals the core of his tragic vision. In fact, this is a statement in which O'Neill's method of constructing his play and his vision meet one another. The circle had been his favorite structural formula ever since his early efforts: yet as late as in this confessional play we see how deeply it was rooted in his personal attitude toward life. Fate is in the circles, in the inescapable repetitions, in the power of the past over the present and over the future. It may shout with the foghorn, too—but the sound has a meaning only to those who are living through the long chain of small, inescapable circles. This is O'Neill's modern artistic approximation to Fate, more personal than his psychological one in *Mourning Becomes Electra*.

The basic motivation for the numerous repetitions in *Long Day's Journey into Night* is given above. Facing the paradox of length once again, we might formulate a question: how many links can one take out of a chain and still make it reach? The more links that are added to a chain, the longer and weightier it becomes; and to those who prefer chains of a smaller calibre, all that can be said is that these are the shackles given to his characters by a tragedian. Some of the repetitions are further motivated by an urge to render ironically conflicting versions of familiar stories at different points of the action and by different characters: Tyrone's picture of Mary's father deviates from that cherished by Mary herself; Mary speaks of her falling in love in contrasting ways. If after these considerations there is still a temptation to abridge, let it happen in small bits, mostly somewhere in the first three acts. It certainly will not do to say in an offhand manner that "there is too much quoting of classic poetry" or that a whole scene is irrelevant.

Long Day's Journey into Night is seen by Mottram as a synthesis of O'Neill's playwriting career. His "earliest one-acters melt into Edmund's sea-voyaging region of dream reality"; there is material from the saloons, utilized even in a group of other plays; *The Straw* is represented by Edmund's tuberculosis; "the Strindbergian elemental family is at last achieved without bogus classicism or pop-Freudianism"; and "the calm of *The Iceman Cometh* comes through again in this last harbour." It is possible to speak of a synthesis from another point of view as well: O'Neill applies here several scenic means of expression he knows thoroughly from previous usages. There is the idea of the fog, expressed mainly through a repetitive sound effect; there are modified monologues, again as the climaxes of the play; there is a continuous circular movement in the dialogue; symbolic significance gradually gathers around one portion of the setting; there are quotations rendering an additional layer of meaning. In a way, the quotations are still another modification of masks: by reciting a poem it is possible for the characters to express feelings not otherwise revealed.

All these means of expression are used in a purposeful way and executed flawlessly within the limits of the style chosen by the playwright: dynamic realism. Even in a play with little or no plot there can be quite a lot of interaction between the scenic images. Besides, *Long Day's Journey into Night* has a plot of an unconventional kind: its action proceeds through the fog into the monologues. Agreeing with Gassner in that "a continuing tension between naturalism and a variety of alternatives of dramatic stylization has characterized the century's theatre" [*Theatre at the Crossroads*], we might call *Long Day's Journey into Night* one of O'Neill's major answers to the challenge created by this tension. It is more than a major answer: it is a masterful one.

"Life in Terms of Lives"

Egil Törnqvist

O'Neill's primary concern was never the depiction of men and women but the depiction of forces at work within men and women. This is what he indicated, when he told Mollan in 1922, that it was just life "as a thing in itself" that interested him, and when he wrote Quinn a few years later, that he was "always trying to interpret Life in terms of lives, never just lives in terms of character." What mattered most to him was not whether individual characters were depicted in a truthful or engaging way, although this was certainly important, but whether the plays evoked a sense of beauty, truth, fate and mystery, whether they constituted "a poetical interpretation and symbolical celebration of life," as he stated in January, 1933. About one of his characters O'Neill once said, that her tragedy consisted in the fact that she could not see the "Oneness of Mankind"; in this she differed from her creator, who constantly stresses the essential oneness of the human race.

This oneness is suggested in two different ways. First, there is the oneness between characters and audience. As we have noted earlier, O'Neill strove to make us feel our "ennobling identity with the tragic figures on the stage." To this end he created characters who on the surface are flesh-and-blood individuals found in their specific situations (for we cannot identify ourselves with abstractions suspended in a void) but whose problems at closer inspection have universal application. Hence, underneath the stoker Yank, the playwright Cape, and the architect Brown we discover Man.

The second aspect will concern us in this chapter: the oneness between

From *A Drama of Souls: Studies in O'Neill's Super-Naturalistic Technique.* © 1968 by Egil Törnqvist. Yale University Press, 1969.

the characters themselves. The struggle between opposing desires, O'Neill sought to show, is fought within most human beings, and the same impulses can be detected in seemingly utterly different characters. Practically, this means that the characters are closely related to one another either because they share similar characteristics, in which case we shall speak of *parallel characters*, or because they find themselves in similar circumstances, in which case we shall speak of *parallel situations*. The two are naturally closely inter-related and cannot be wholly kept apart.

Blatant or disguised antitheses can be found in any play, and critics have usually paid much attention to the polar aspect and what it enfolds. But whereas contrast, pure and simple, belongs to the black-and-white world of melodrama, higher forms of drama prefer to have it operate in close conjunction with parallelism. This is perhaps most apparent in the Shakespearean subplot, which both contrasts with and parallels and main action. Just as, in this case, the contrast is immediately recognizable and represents a surface level, whereas the parallel holds true on a much deeper level, never discovered, we may rest assured, by the multitude of Shake-speare's audience, so, with O'Neill, the parallels tend to operate on a deeper, more obscure level than the contrasts. . . .

Parallel Characters

In a tightly composed, structurally conventional play like [*Long Day's Journey into Night*] we find several parallel characters appearing only in the dialogue. Thus, during the long talk between Edmund and Tyrone in the final act both cannot help drawing attention to painful parallel cases. "Booze and consumption" killed Dowson and Mary's father—as it may Edmund. And Dante Gabriel Rossetti "was a dope fiend"—like Mary. The very things that should not be mentioned *are* mentioned, because the char-acters cannot get away from themselves; even when talking about other things, they keep thinking about their own fate; and the slips are illustra-tions of their spiritual isolation; in a minor figure they parallel the more serious blows the Tyrones deal to one another, for rightly considered these too are slips, illustrative of their inability to transcend their isolation and their past. These parallels, together with others (the suicide of Tyrone's father as compared to the suicide attempts of Edmund and Mary; Cathleen's uncle, who drank himself to death as Jamie doubtless will do), provide a dark, fateful backdrop for the drama of the Tyrones and widen its scope; they turn, as it were, the domestic drama into a universal tragedy.

Other parallels, more amply dealt with in the play, have meanings beyond this basic one. Here again we are confronted with figures symbolizing tendencies within the pivotal character, Mary Tyrone. There is, for example, the somewhat surprising resemblance between Mary and Fat Violet, the prostitute at whose breast Jamie seeks consolation. The obvious and glaring contrast between Violet and Mary, the whore and the "virgin," the woman of all men and the woman of no man (for this is what Mary's name and dream of becoming a nun amount to), is levelled out by a more basic similarity. Thus, in her first speech Mary points out that she has "gotten too fat," and it is pointed out that Jamie likes fat women but that he finds Violet too fat. Both women play the piano. Violet has been "on drunks" lately, as Mary has relapsed into morphinism; and Jamie brings the two together in his remark that before he discovered his mother's addiction, he could not imagine "that any women but whores took dope"; in a sense, his mother thus appears as a whore to him; by not loving him enough, by hiding in her dope world, she betrays him, makes him forever hunger for love. Yet Mary too hungers for love; and so does Violet. Both feel lonely, unpopular; Mary lacks friends; customers do not fall for Vi. Both hope to be loved despite their deformities, Violet despite her fatness, Mary despite her deficiencies as a wife and mother. As soon as Jamie knows that the beloved mother has left him forever, he goes to sleep with Violet. He believes that he selects her out of consideration for a fellow bum. What he does not see is that his concern for Violet is motivated by her resemblance to Mary, that she functions as an admittedly unsuccessful mother substitute. Thus Jamie's visit to Mamie Burns' brothel becomes a pathetic illustration of his inability to get away from the mother; his love will follow her still.

Even closer is the parallel between Mary and Bridget, the cook. The fog affects Bridget's rheumatism as it does Mary's. And she appears to be as much of a whiskey addict as Mary is a "dope fiend." Their desperation, made acute—or rather symbolized—by their bodily pain, stems, as in the case of Violet, from an intense feeling of loneliness. In act 1 Bridget, who needs company, keeps Mary in the kitchen for a long while with "lies about her relations." In act 2 Mary keeps Cathleen in the living room with memories of her own happy past which, according to Tyrone, must be taken "with a grain of salt." She too needs a listener.

Cathleen describes Bridget as little better than a maniac, who cannot stand being left alone:

She's like a raging divil. She'll bite my head off.

If she don't get something to quiet her temper, she'll be after me with a cleaver.

If we are reminded here of Ella Harris in *Chillun*, the association is apt, for Ella, like Mary, seems modelled to a great extent on O'Neill's mother.

Hence Bridget, being another Ella, is seen to be another Mary. Never appearing but always (since we are constantly reminded of her presence in the dialogue and in the exits to the kitchen) lurking in the background, she comes to personify the reckless, destructive impulse within Mary, which finally "kills" her three men. Mary says:

> It's no use finding fault with Bridget. She doesn't listen. I can't threaten her, or she'd threaten she'd leave. And she does do her best at times. It's too bad they seem to be just the times you're sure to be late, James. Well, there's this consolation: it's difficult to tell from her cooking whether she's doing her best or her worst.

This is no doubt a disguised self-portrait and a speech of defense. In her marriage Mary claims to have "done the best [she] could—under the circumstances." She is no more suited for it than Bridget is for cooking. And besides, Tyrone has never given her much of a chance; he has never really understood that just as you cannot expect the food to taste good if you are late for it, so you can't expect a woman to be a good wife unless you give her a proper environment, which she can delight in. Such is Mary's defensive view; hidden beneath it is her other, more deeply felt view that she is herself to blame. It is precisely because she feels so guilty that Mary cannot accept any blame; she refutes it, like Bridget, by not listening and by eventually "leaving" her family.

PARALLEL SITUATIONS

In *Journey* O'Neill has inserted what to a casual observer may seem a digression out of tune with the serious mood of the play and completely unrelated to it. I refer to the Harker-Shaughnessy episode, which fascinated O'Neill to the extent that he used it again and more extensively in *Misbegotten*.

Shaughnessy is a poor Irish tenant on a farm owned by Tyrone. This farm borders on the estate belonging to Harker, a Yankee Standard Oil millionaire. Edmund has just met Shaughnessy and he is reporting what the tenant has told him:

> (*Grins at his father provocatively.*) Well, you remember, Papa, the ice pond on Harker's estate is right next to the farm, and you remember Shaughnessy keeps pigs. Well, it seems there's a break in the fence and the pigs have been bathing in the millionaire's ice pond, and Harker's foreman told him he was sure Shaugh-

nessy had broken the fence on purpose to give his pigs a free wallow.

But when Harker came to rebuke Shaughnessy, the Irishman

accused Harker of making his foreman break down the fence to entice the pigs into the ice pond in order to destroy them. The poor pigs, Shaughnessy yelled, had caught their death of cold. Many of them were dying of pneumonia, and several others had been taken down with cholera from drinking the poisoned water.

This anecdote obviously helps to characterize the Tyrones in the sense that their reactions to it reveal something about their natures. Tyrone's reaction is especially illuminating; while he spontaneously sides with Shaughnessy, he gives some half-hearted support to Harker. But the story is also, I would suggest, the story of the Tyrone family in disguise. Thus the poor farm bordering on the rich estate illustrates Tyrone's transition from poverty to wealth. It is clear that he shares characteristics with both combatants—hence his divided sympathies. He is of humble Irish origin like Shaughnessy, who nevertheless claims that he would be a "King of Ireland," if he had his rights, a claim that would not be foreign to Tyrone, judging by his name and pride in the old country. Like Harker, he is a well-to-do "businessman" and landowner; Harker is ironically referred to as a "king of America," and Tyrone has acquired a similar position as a nation-wide matinée idol. While accumulating his wealth and rising in society Tyrone has declined from "King" to "king," from Ireland to America, from Shakespeare to Monte Cristo, from artist to businessman. Like the pigs, he has run away from the poor farm to the rich estate, but in the process he has fatally poisoned himself. Mary too has moved outside her fenced-in, innocent childhood environment with the same result. Both of them find that they can no longer call their souls their own.

Many of the pigs, we learn, die of pneumonia after they have caught cold. Edmund is, for a long time, thought to suffer from a summer cold—until it is disclosed that he is affected by a far more fatal disease: consumption. Other pigs die from drinking the poisoned ice water. Tyrone's father died by, perhaps deliberately, mistaking "rat poison for flour." Tyrone himself early began poisoning his sons by giving them whiskey as medicine, thereby laying a foundation for future alcoholism. During the long day we actually see the three men "wallow" in whiskey and ice water to make life bearable and short. Mary was poisoned by the quack who first gave her morphine; Tyrone constantly refers to the morphine as "the poison." Jamie jealously "poisoned" Eugene with measles (from which the baby died) and Edmund with "worldly wisdom"—hard drinking and Broadway tarts—when he was merely a boy.

Although it is never made completely clear, it is strongly implied that it was Shaughnessy who broke down the fence. Poor as he is, he wants to give his pigs "a free wallow" at the expense of the hated Yankee millionaire; thus we may construe his motives. But the cheap bath has, as we have seen, consequences unforeseen by the tenant. In the same way Tyrone, unable to unlearn his childhood lesson of "the value of a dollar," tries to get everything second hand and as a result works destruction on his family. It was the cheap quack he sent Mary to that got her started on morphine. And it is a cheap sanatorium, "endowed by a group of millionaire factory owners, for the benefit of their workers," to which he finally decides to send Edmund; and the son evidently stands as slim a chance of survival there as do the pigs in Harker's ice pond. The choice the-poor-Irish-boy-in-Tyrone makes is the choice Shaughnessy would have made; it is motivated not merely by an excessive money consciousness but also by a wish to benefit, for once, from the plutocrats, who had treated Tyrone and his family as little better than slaves; Tyrone's sanatorium plan is thus in a sense another battle fought against the Yankees.

Shaughnessy's violent attack on Harker, blaming him for what he himself has most likely done, may be seen as a grotesque and simplified version of the way each of the Tyrones react with regard to the major "crimes" committed in the past. It is precisely when they feel most guilty that they blame others, applying Shaughnessy's technique of attacking before being attacked; he who evokes their guilt-feelings immediately turns into an enemy against whom they must defend themselves; their attacks thus stem primarily from a need to relieve themselves from an acute self-hatred.

Yet the fact that the question "Who broke down the fence that opened the way for the pigs' destruction?" is not unequivocally answered is of some significance. No doubt O'Neill was unwilling to provide a clear answer because he was aware that the question foreshadows the much larger one we ask ourselves at the end of the play: "Who is to blame for the destruction of the Tyrone family?" The whole play, in a sense, is devoted to answering this question. The web of guilt is so complex, is distributed to so many hands and stretches so far back in time that, although we realize that all the Tyrones have their share in it, and Tyrone perhaps most of all, we are ultimately left with Mary's philosophy that life, rather than any one of them, must carry the heaviest responsibility.

Structurally, the pig story springs naturally from the form chosen by O'Neill for his play. The technique of gradual revelation strictly adhered to in *Journey* prevents overt references to the family fate in the early acts; the play structure itself is designed as a long journey into the dark interior of the family and its individual members. The dramatist is obviously presented with a problem here. For the sake of dramatic suspense he is forced to make his characters withhold important information, while for the sake of structural unity he is forced to make them deliver it. He must therefore make the dialogue in the early acts function on (at least) two levels. Even if we do not—and, in fact, often cannot—grasp its more profound meaning at a first reading / hearing, we frequently sense that what the characters are saying is of a greater significance than it appears to be at the moment when it is presented; and we axiomatically assume that some of it will be made clear in the process of the play. This awareness of as of yet unintelligible levels creates a feeling of suspense, which piques our interest before it has been stirred by the human drama before us.

The parallel includes a marked contrast in *tone* between the anecdote and the ensuing action, which illustrates its meaning. The Tyrones can laugh at the Shaughnessy episode precisely because they do not realize that it is their own story in disguise. Had it been told at the end of the long day they—and we—would doubtless view it differently. Thus, by changing the perspective, O'Neill illustrates how life, depending on our degree of involvement, can be seen either as a farce or as a tragedy.

The pigs-in-the-ice-pond episode appears again—and more emphatically—in *Misbegotten*, where Phil Hogan plays the same trick on Harder that Shaughnessy does on Harker in *Journey*. Phil and Josie, as their surname indicates, are not unlike their pigs. When the play opens Hogan is down by the pigpen—"where he belongs, the old hog," his hostile son comments, and Phil's appearance bears him out:

> *He has a thick neck, lumpy, sloping shoulders, a barrel-like trunk, stumpy legs, and big feet. His arms are short and muscular, with large hairy hands. His head is round with thinning sandy hair. His face is fat with a snub nose, long upper lip, big mouth, and little blue eyes with bleached lashes and eyebrows that remind one of a white pig's.*

Josie's outward appearance—she weighs "*around one hundred and eighty*"—and her boast that she has slept with every man in the neighborhood make her seemingly a "pig" of a woman. When Phil proudly calls his pigs "fine ambitious American-born pigs," which "don't miss any opportunities," he is actually describing himself and his daughter, "two of a kind," constantly scheming against the Yankees. As they doctor up a sick pig "to look good for a day or two"—long enough to be sold at a good price—so they are in the habit of dressing Josie up to look good to soften the landlord, when he comes around to demand his rent. And as Phil helps his pigs to stroll into the millionaire's grounds, where they can "wallow happily along the shores of the ice pond," so he also attempts to help Josie exchange the "lousy farm" for Jim Tyrone's estate, where she could live "in ease and comfort."

Josie at one point—the early part of act 3—attempts to perform the action of the pigs. Believing that Jim has been treacherous and intends to sell the farm to the hated neighbor, she is prepared to defend her home and blackmail Jim by offering him her body and then to force him to marry her and in this manner "enter" his estate. But it is clear from the beginning that the role does not fit her: the low scheme is not hers but her "virtuous" brother's; she has the best excuse possible for prostituting herself at this point: not only is it a matter of saving her own and her father's home and of taking revenge on one who has not kept his word; apart from and despite all this, Josie is in love with Jim—hence, sleeping with him is her heart's desire. The scheming role is repugnant to her, and it is significant that she cannot force herself to kiss Jim "*passionately*" until this role has been dropped and love alone motivates her actions. Thus Josie, even when attempting the "pig" role, is shown to fail miserably in adopting it. For a brief, blissful moment she believes that she and Jim can find love and happiness together. Then she discovers that he is "dead," that the little part of him that is still living is haunted by the memory of the mother and of the sin he has committed against her. She gives him the night of tender, innocent, maternal love he asks for, a self-sacrificing love, "the greatest of all," she remarks, "because it costs so much." Josie thus runs the gamut from (partly) calculating, prostitute-like love through genuine passion to spiritualized love and servitude. Her pig-like characteristics, it turns out, are merely the outward "mask" protecting her romantic, virginal soul. The moment Jim admits his genuine love for her, she drops this "mask." Never acting like a "pig," her fate is quite the opposite of that of the animals. When dawn comes she is still a virgin, still unpoisoned, facing a new day of hard work on the poor farm rather than the deathly "ease and comfort" of the rich estate. Phil, too, is capable of a tender, unselfish love beneath his rough, materialistic surface. His true reason for bringing Jim and Josie together is not so much land hunger as a desire to see his daughter happily married to a man he likes; as Phil expresses it: "I'm not a pig that has no other thought but eating!"

The true counterpart of the pigs is the prostitute Jim slept with on the train carrying his mother's corpse eastwards; he significantly always refers to her as the "pig"; finds her come-on smile "as cold as a polar bear's feet"—a simile that relates her to the ice pond; and gets "a bad taste" in his mouth, when he thinks of his experience with her a year earlier, just as Harder is said to deplore "the taste of pig in next summer's ice water." The pigs, which stroll into the estate, happily wallow along the shores of the ice pond, and then die of cold or cholera from the "dirty water," have their human parallel in this "fat blonde pig" who, wallowing in bed with Jim Tyrone, heir to an estate, "for fifty bucks a night," is already frozen and poisoned to death by a life devoid of love. Outwardly resembling Josie, she is actually her antithesis: as Josie incarnates the life force, so the prostitute represents death-in-life. Unable to feel anything for the dead mother, Jim concluded that he too had "died," the inference being that he could not survive the loss of maternal love. He logically proceeds to seek the company of someone who is as damned and "dead" as he is, a whore with "parlor house written all over her" and "a face like an overgrown doll's" —heavily made up, that is, and artificially young-looking like the dead mother. In the prostitute he seeks at once a mother substitute and revenge on the mother for deserting him, both love and "the suicide of love" to use Michael Cape's definition of the prostitute in *Welded*, both life and death.

The Door and the Mirror

Travis Bogard

Mrs. O'Neill's diary for June 21, 1939, contains what is possibly the first recorded mention of another play [O'Neill] planned whose subject was his family and whose title was *Long Day's Journey into Night*. The play was begun shortly after the completion of *The Iceman Cometh* and, together with *Hughie*, was O'Neill's major creative effort of 1940. It was completed in September. Then, after a period of illness, he turned to its sequel, *A Moon for the Misbegotten*. He had written half of the first draft of that play when the Japanese bombed Pearl Harbor. O'Neill wrote to Dudley Nichols on December 16, 1941, that he had managed to finish the draft, but that the heart had gone out of its writing. Although he worked on it sporadically through 1943 and during the same period made revisions of *A Touch of the Poet* and developed the scenario of *The Last Conquest*, O'Neill's career as a playwright ended as the United States entered the war. By 1943, the tremor in his hand made sustained work impossible.

His illness and the war were real reasons for silence, but equally important was an underlying cause: having written the two plays about his family, O'Neill had no further place to go. *Long Day's Journey into Night* was the play he had been trying to write from the outset of his career; its achievement was his raison d'être as an artist. *A Moon for the Misbegotten* was an essential coda, an act of love, of charity and of contrition. Mrs. O'Neill recorded movingly what happened to O'Neill as he wrote. His work day was a long one, five hours in the morning and additional hours in the

From *Contour in Time: The Plays of Eugene O'Neill.* © 1972 by Oxford University Press.

afternoon. As she described him, he was a man "being tortured every day by his own writing. He would come out of his study at the end of a day gaunt and sometimes weeping. His eyes would be all red and he looked ten years older than when he went in in the morning." O'Neill said not without irony that he was writing plays he knew he could finish, but the Tyrone plays were more than substitutes for the cycle. A lifetime's psychological and physical pressures had cornered him at last. It was a moment for truth and he told it.

When it was said, he was not entirely certain that it had emerged as truth. Edmund Tyrone, having told his father of all that has meaning for him, concludes his account of his quest by saying, "I couldn't touch what I tried to tell you just now. I just stammered. That's the best I'll ever do. . . . Well it will be faithful realism, at least. Stammering is the native eloquence of us fog-people." He was wrong. *Long Day's Journey into Night* is not the work of a stammerer, but of a man who had become a master of his art, and whose native speech—not the words only, but the full acted drama— had the eloquence of a poet. The technical experimentation of the 1920s often caused him to beat frenetically against the limits of the stage. In the last four plays, the stage did all he asked of it without strain. The result is the highest achievement of the American realistic theatre.

What he asks is deceptively simple. Ironically, O'Neill's ultimate "experiment" was a return to four boards and a passion—to in other words, a confident reliance on his actors. He, who had gone to such elaborate lengths to ensure that his actors would fulfill his purposes, loading them with masks, asides, choral support and an infinity of pauses, now removed all exterior pressures. He was still generous with stage directions suggesting intonation and attitude, but he no longer tried to enforce a performance with the impedimenta of the Art Theatre. Everything, now, is in the role. An actor in these plays cannot hide behind personal mannerisms, clever business or habitual stage trickery. O'Neill has stripped all but the most minimal requirements from the stage, leaving the actors naked. They must play or perish.

Essentially, what is needed as setting for the four last plays are table surfaces and chairs. Properties are few, mostly bottles and glasses. Costume requirements are negligible. The most elaborate of the plays is *The Iceman Cometh*, which requires the bar structure and the essentials of the birthday feast, but even these are minimal in view of the play's length and the size of its cast. What O'Neill makes from his simple materials is extraordinary. In the printed texts, he describes in elaborate detail each of the settings, listing titles of books on the shelves, giving the history of Hope's saloon and the hotel where Erie lives. It is information that he provides but does not insist on. An actor should know it, but an audience will perceive such details only through the filter of performance. It is said of Shakespeare that when he wishes the details of his setting to be specific, he makes it possible for the actor to show them. The same, despite the very different theatrical conventions, can be said of O'Neill in the last plays.

What an audience learns is surprisingly detailed, considering the limited means. The house of the Tyrones, its environment and the historical period are confidently set forth. Although the setting is bare, the audience knows that the house has four bedrooms and an attic and a cellar, that there is a big lawn ending in a hedge by the street, that the sea is near and that the town is a long streetcar ride away. The importance of the house to the action is evident, but it is through the action that the setting is fully evoked. So for the period. In creating the historical time for the two Tyrone plays, 1912 and 1923, O'Neill has relied on few specific historical details. The sinking of the *Titanic* or the arrival of Scott at the South Pole in 1912 might well have provided imagery for the desperately isolated Tyrones. The point, however, is that they *are* isolated, and no superficial references to period are needed to testify to the fact that they live in a society that is not very complex, in which they can find such privacy. By comparison, the world of *A Moon for the Misbegotten* is difficult, involved with new economic realities that Hogan resists as the post-war boom overruns his individualism. O'Neill has felt the difference, conveyed it in each line and attitude and has needed nothing more elaborate to evoke the period.

Like the details of setting and the historical period the time-scheme of *Long Day's Journey into Night* is simple and placed in the grain of the action without special technical elaboration. In many earlier plays, O'Neill pretended that the carefully designed, detailed planning of the progress of time had meaning. Occasionally, as with the sunset-to-dawn pattern of *Lazarus Laughed*, a somewhat gratuitous symbolism was achieved, but more often, the time structure was arbitrary and vague in its significance.

The arrangement of time in the autobiographical plays, however, is anything but arbitrary or extraneous. Around the time plan, O'Neill marshals such "effects" as he uses. Both plays begin in the full light of day to the sound of laughter. In *Long Day's Journey into Night*, as the Tyrones enter from the dining room, laughter sounds gently. Sun pours through the windows, the fog and the sound of the foghorn that has kept the family awake through the night have gone. The moment is poised and normal, but almost at once O'Neill denies its normalcy and starts the progression that had been a hallmark of his style from the first work he did for the theatre. The light dwindles, the fog returns, the foghorn sounds again. Gradually, the space diminishes to the area defined by a single light bulb over the central table in the room. The Tyrones' world is seen in its barest essentials. The proposition is clear, both to the actors and their characters: if life is to be created it must be evolved from the simple elements in this limited space. There are no extraneous symbols—isolating actors in follow-spots, diminishing the room by pulling in the walls of the set. Everything is in the action as the fog becomes the physical evidence of the isolation of the Tyrones.

The view of human nature set forth in the plays is of divided beings— the conception that earlier occasioned O'Neill's use of masks and other devices to suggest outer and inner lives. The Tyrones, however, need no masks. In their nearly mortal extremity, they have nothing to hide. Their pain fills their being so completely that their essential natures lie close to the surface. Thus Tyrone's charm, his friendliness and grace have worn thin under the erosion of despair. His actor's carriage and voice are ingrained in his demeanor, but as the night wears on and as the whiskey sickens him without making him drunk, the hidden man comes clearly into view. Jamie's cynical mask is dropped as the whiskey begins to talk, permitting the defenseless child in him to be seen. In the same way, as Mary descends farther into the doped state, the young girl alive within the pain-wracked woman comes forth to haunt them all. Whiskey and morphine effectively remove all disguise.

The words that come when the masks are off are in the form of soliloquies and monologues such as were from the first a characteristic of O'Neill's playwriting. Now, however, there is no breaking of the play's realistic limits. When, for example, Mary is left alone at the end of the scene with Cathleen in act 2, she speaks of her past in a long monologue that arises naturally from her addiction. As the morphine takes effect it causes her to babble, but she is still sufficiently aware not to be entirely dulled to her condition. Her words rise involuntarily out of her loneliness and guilt and speak of her longing for the life of the girl she was. It is as if she speaks to the girl in the past so as to assuage the loneliness of the present. Similarly, the long monologues of Edmund and his father in act 4 evoke the past as the only surcease from the doped present. Over their words there hangs no hint of Art Theatre Show Shop. O'Neill has enabled his actors to motivate the monologues and make them convincingly natural, psychologically real.

The two Tyrone plays hold firmly to the best realistic theatre practice. Yet for all their "faithful realism," it should be remarked that the dramas more readily than many earlier works approach the abstraction and symbolism so characteristic of the expressionist mode. The quality and force of that abstraction is difficult to define. O'Neill does not try to convince his audiences that the world of the Tyrones is a microcosm, as he suggested with the typified chorus of *The Iceman Cometh*. The Tyrones and the Hogans are particular people, moving in a specific time, facing highly individual problems. Like many other works of the realistic American theatre — *Come Back, Little Sheba* or *A Hatful of Rain*, for example — the plays are contained and domestic, well-told case histories. Yet to call *Long Day's Journey into Night* a "domestic tragedy" is to underestimate seriously its emotional effect. It is enlarged, not in the sense of Aristotelian "heightening," but more by its unremitting movement "behind life," in the phrase O'Neill once used to describe Strindberg's expressionist dramas. For a play to move "behind life" means that it expands inward, through the surfaces, and toward the core of life itself. The inner enlargement of the Tyrone plays not only scrutinize the motives that produce the painful events, but somehow, also, they enlarge an audience's knowledge of the suffering these events produce. No drama of modern times contains more of pain's substance than *Long Day's Journey into Night*, but in the final analysis, it is not the events, shocking though they are, that grip the audience. The Tyrones suffer and the spectators are convinced that when suffering is the only reality, life is truly as it is depicted in the play.

Verisimilitude does not necessarily lead to a universal statement. However, when *Long Day's Journey into Night* is played, another dimension opens. In the theatre, the suffering of the playwright is more real, if that is possible, than that of his characters. The audience shares them both, and moves as in a dream that is both real and more than real along the course of this "Wander Play." Pain exists in a double layer, one that can seem a fiction, one that must be a truth as the truth of suffering has seldom been stated. An emotion appropriate to an aesthetic experience and an emotion evoked by reality join to create in the spectators a capacity for pity that extends well beyond the boundaries of the theatre and rises to an acknowledgment of exceptional purity: that the universality of pain makes pity and understanding and forgiveness the greatest of human needs.

At their climactic moments, both the Tyrone plays convey the qualities of a dream. The fog or moonlight, the whiskey or dope causes the characters to drift in slow emotional movements. Activity ceases, and each play becomes "a play for voices" that permits the lyrics of lamentation and loss to be heard clearly. Physical objects are only the source of reverie. Edmund and his father play cards. A bottle and glasses are on the table and above it an electric chandelier. Only these have substance in the room. The two men sit in near darkness and silence. A card is played or a drink is poured or a light bulb is turned on. Something in the outer world is touched, but it is a meaningless gesture. Then, as the object is touched, the mind recoils, moving away from that physical contact with the present into the past, wandering in a reverie that is as formless and far-reaching as the night outside. The reverie ended, the ballooning thought returns to the space where life is. Something else is touched; reverie begins again, in a movement that is like a man's swimming, sinking and touching bottom in order to rise up again into the currents of the water. In such scenes, time as an adjunct of reality has stopped; forward motion has ended. The slow turning of memory is the play's only action. Life becomes a dream of pain.

What the morphine brings to the surface in Mary Tyrone is awareness of the isolation that is both her need and her terror. As she appears in the first scene of the play, although small hints of what is to follow quickly become apparent, she seems a woman to whom her home and family are all, as they were to Essie Miller in *Ah, Wilderness!* The dependence of the men on her is marked, and not only in their concern for her health. She emerges in the few moments of normalcy as the source of life for them, the quiet hub around which they move, happy in her presence. The summer house seems to be truly a home, and the comforts it offers, though modest, are sufficient to their well-being. The illusion of the home is an essential image to establish at the outset, for it, of course, is not what it seems. The room is shabby, poorly furnished, a temporary residence at best. It is like the cheap hotels of Tyrone's road tours, where Mary has waited alone, unable to associate with theatre people, spending nights in idleness until her husband comes or is brought home from the theatre. Mary's life has taught her loneliness and provided her with the definition of a home as a place where "one is never lonely." She remembers having had in her girlhood a "real" home, yet the memory is illusory. Idealizing her father, she has obliterated whatever faults existed in him. Tyrone tells Edmund her home was an ordinary one and her father a steady drinker. His implied question is whether Mary's girlhood was indeed the happy time she remembers it to have been. O'Neill makes clear that her desire, even as a girl, was to escape into a lonely world—into the convent where she could be sustained by a vision and live a simple, virginal existence. That Mary loves her husband admits no question, yet in a larger sense, love has disturbed her spirit and violated her desire to retain her encapsuled purity. Love has led her into a world for which she was not and never could be ready. She needs to be alone in a protected silence. She blames her failure vaguely on life, and she is right to do so. She says,

> None of us can help the things life has done to us. They're done before you realize it, and once they're done they make you do other things until at last everything comes between you and what you'd like to be, and you've lost your true self forever.

In seeking her "true self," Mary is looking for a self that does not exist. Repeatedly she remarks that she cannot find her glasses and therefore cannot see to fix her hair. In other words, she cannot see what she is. She associates her Catholicism loosely with her need for morphine. Morphine is medicine to still the pain in her arthritic hands; the hands once played the piano; she studied music in the convent. "I had two dreams. To be a nun, that was the more beautiful one. To become a concert pianist, that was the other." But the dreams of lost faith and spent talent are dreams of escape which affect her as the morphine does by pulling her from the present, from the house, from the irony of Tyrone's buying property without providing a home, and from her indifference that is like hatred of her family.

In the course of the play, Mary shifts repeatedly from a young girl to a cynical embittered, self-contemptuous creature. Her guilt at failing to take care of her dead child, Eugene, is translated into insane hatred of her husband: "I know why he wants to send you to a sanatorium," she tells Edmund. "To take you away from me! He's always tried to do that. He's been jealous of every one of my babies! He kept finding ways to make me leave them. That's what caused Eugene's death. He's been jealous of you most of all. He knew I loved you best because —" Frantically babying Edmund does not prevent her from blaming him for being born and starting her on the dope habit. Edmund is her scourge and should never have been born. Her hatred of Jamie is less ambiguous. Jamie's need for her is by no means reciprocated. She hates his cynicism, turns from him in fear that he will discover her need of the dope and silently accuses him of murdering the dead child. When the morphine talks in her, she treats her husband with a mixture of love and contempt, dwelling on his failures and yet maintaining the truth of her love for him. As Deborah Harford escaped in her dreams, Mary needs to turn from them all, to find a path that will take her deep into the fog, hating the loneliness, yet wanting to be rid of the obligations the men's love place upon her. Edmund describes the blank wall she builds around herself:

> It's . . . like a bank of fog in which she hides and loses herself. Deliberately, that's the hell of it! You know something in her does it deliberately—to get beyond our reach, to be rid of us, to forget we're alive! It's as if, in spite of loving us, she hated us!

Mary's refusal of all her responsibilities has bred in her a guilt she is incapable of bearing. The morphine must be used to wipe out "the pain— *all* the pain—I mean in my hands." In the morphine trance, she moves gently back in time, seeking to re-create the illusions of a happier world, before there was a past to make her what she has become. Her wedding dress, like Con Melody's red uniform, is a symbol of something that never was a substantial reality. Her quest is for a hope lost, a goalless search for salvation never to be attained.

The men around Mary are condemned as she is to hopeless questing. Her husband like Con Melody is both poet and peasant. Under the graceful bearing of the aging actor, trained to eradicate the brogue, to gesture and speak with authority, there lies the fear of the poverty-stricken past. O'Neill has falsified to a degree the penny-pinching qualities in his father in drawing Tyrone, yet the fear his father felt was undoubtedly a real one, as was the sense he expressed of having failed his potential as an actor. Like Mary, Tyrone is doomed to an endless life of regret for something lost in the past, holding to a hope that has no reality. "What the hell was it I wanted to buy?" he asks, and there is no answer unless it is protection and the quieting of irrational fears. His failure as an artist and as a husband had made him guilty beyond pardon. Like a lugged bear he stands as the target for all of his family's recriminations. Yet, perhaps more than any of the others, he shoulders the responsibilities of their lives. He has kindness in him, and a devotion to his wife that overrides all her animosity. For Edmund he demonstrates little close feeling. A generalized, somewhat distant affection is the most he reveals for his younger son. For Jamie, however, he has a strong feeling that is so positive it can turn easily into hostility. The two months during which Mary has returned to normal he describes to Jamie as "heaven," and he adds, "This home has been a home again. But I needn't tell you, Jamie." O'Neill amplifies the sense of understanding with a stage direction:

> *His son looks at him, for the first time with an understanding sympathy. It is as if suddenly a deep bond of common feeling existed between them in which their antagonisms could be forgotten.*

It is Jamie's sobbing in the final moments of the play that breaks Tyrone, and Jamie who evokes in him his only shows of violence and perhaps also his most bitter expression of sorrow. As his son lies drunk and unconscious he says with sadness,

> A sweet spectacle for me! My first-born, who I hoped would bear my name in honor and dignity, who showed such brilliant promise!

Tyrone, more than any other member of the family, honors the bonds of the home. He is capable of love but is often driven toward hatred. Even so, he never truly hates, but lives isolated within the frame of the bond, attempting to love in spite of everything. He turns from the pain of his life, to the local barroom; he buys bad real estate to purchase security he cannot find; he drinks to dope his mind to the point of forgetfulness. But he does not betray. He remains a simple man, free of cynicism, incapable of hatred. O'Neill's view of his father contains full charity.

O'Neill's picture of his younger self and of his brother Jamie is on the surface clear enough. Jamie, like his brother and father, is lost, embittered and cynical, wanting his mother whose rejection of him perhaps reaches farther back than the time when morphine forced her into drugged isolation. To compensate for her loss, he has sought to destroy himself with the profligate life of the Broadway rounder, and he has attempted to corrupt his brother, in the pretense of "putting him wise" to women and liquor. In Jamie, pain can have no anodyne. Liquor, far from dulling his loss, makes it unbearable, and, while Edmund is fussed over, even babied, no one tries to help Jamie. Nor is escape possible. Edmund can move into the fog—as he does in the third act—and find a kind of peace. The peace of belonging to a secret at the source of life, "the vision of beatitude" which he attempts to describe to his father, offers him a way out, just as Mary's dream of finding her girlhood faith and Tyrone's memory of Booth's praise have power to assuage the present. There is no vision of beatitude for Jamie in *Long Day's Journey into Night*. His need is always beside him, in Mary, but he cannot reach her. Like Tantalus, he has no refuge from desire. His is the howl of a soul lost in hell.

Edmund, as O'Neill presents him, is clearly drawn, and, as a dramatic character, offers adequate material to an actor, but there is perhaps less truth in his portrait than in the others. He is a strangely neutral figure, except in the scene with his father in act 4. Even there he speaks out of a solitude that is unlike the isolation of the others. Although O'Neill has been at pains to show what the past has made his parents and brother, it is unclear what the past has made Edmund. O'Neill perhaps understandably suppresses the fact of his brief marriage and his child and omits the crucial event in 1912 of his divorce. He mentions that Edmund has been to sea, and almost perfunctorily adds that he has lived in the sewers of New York and Buenos Aires and has attempted suicide. None of these events, except insofar as his having been to sea conditions his vision of belonging, bear heavily on what he is. He seems to be the victim of the family, unwanted, betrayed, led astray by his brother and, now, with tuberculosis, suffering under his father's penuriousness. It is easy—perhaps too easy—to sympathize with

Edmund. He is no more than an embittered adolescent, certainly a pale copy of what Eugene O'Neill was at that time.

How deliberate the suppression of personal qualities was is difficult to estimate. In *A Moon for the Misbegotten*, Jamie's brother is mentioned, but many descriptions of his reactions to Jamie's behavior were deleted in final revision. For example a speech of Jamie's in act 3, reads in the printed text, "Don't want to touch me now, eh? (*He shrugs his shoulders mechanically.*) Sorry. I'm a damned fool. I shouldn't have told you." In the typescript the speech contains a canceled reference to Jamie's brother:

> Don't want to touch me now? Well, I don't blame you. Except you promised. No, forget that. But you didn't know what you were letting yourself in for. My fault. I shouldn't have told you. Too rotten and horrible. Never told anyone except my brother. He said "You dirty bastard"—then tried to excuse me because we'd always been such close pals—blamed it all on booze. He knows the booze game from his own experience—the mad things you do. All the same he couldn't forget. He loved her, too. He's never felt the same about me since. Tries to. He's a pal. But can't. Makes excuses to himself to keep away from me. For another reason, too. Can't keep me from seeing that he knows what I'm up against, and that there's only one answer. He knows it's hopeless. He can't help wishing I were dead, too—for my sake. (*Rousing himself, with a shrug of his shoulders— self-contemptuously.*) Nuts! Why do I tell you about him. Nothing to do with you. (*Sneering.*) A little more sob stuff.

The responses of Jamie's brother in the second play are justifiably deleted. Whatever reticence O'Neill may have felt in describing his reactions to his brother's behavior, his views are irrelevant to the moment in the play. However, the elimination of detail about his own character in *Long Day's Journey into Night* is of another order. Edmund's somewhat poetic inclinations to lose himself in the fog and his desire to enter into a state of Dionysian ecstasy are recognizable characteristics of the young playwright as his early plays showed him to be. Such melancholy, mingled with narcissism, is little more than a normal stage of the developing adolescent ego. Yet, in this connection, one anecdote of the year 1912 is important.

It is an account by a nurse, Olive Evans, who cared for O'Neill shortly before he entered the sanatorium:

> Olive thought him vain because he was constantly studying himself in the bureau mirror and finally asked whether he would

like the bureau moved to where he could see himself while in bed. "After I did it," she recalls, "I told him, 'Now you can see your madonna eyes,' and he looked shy and pleased. He had heavenly eyes, the most beautiful I've ever seen. So did Mrs. O'Neill—large, dark, dreamy eyes."

(Louis Sheaffer, O'Neill, Son and Playwright)

How much may be read from the anecdote is uncertain, but the later remark to George Cram Cook, who had taxed him for continually looking in mirrors, should be remembered. When a man says he looks into mirrors to be sure he is there, the habit may indicate more than simple vanity. Con Melody's need to posture before the mirror to bolster his ego and his dreams is not much removed from O'Neill's need of the mirror to maintain his identity. *Long Day's Journey into Night* is a mirror, the last into which O'Neill looked, and it is of concern to explore what he found there when, for once, he committed himself to see himself unmasked and clear.

The characters most unambiguously drawn as self-portraits are the Poet in *Fog*, John Brown in *Bread and Butter*, Robert Mayo in *Beyond the Horizon*, Stephen Murray in *The Straw*, Michael Cape in *Welded*, Dion Anthony in *The Great God Brown*, Richard Miller in *Ah, Wilderness!* John in *Days without End*, Simon Harford in *More Stately Mansions* and Edmund Tyrone in *Long Day's Journey into Night*. The physical portrait of each is that of a sensitive man, with big, wide-set dark eyes, a high forehead, dark hair brushed straight back, a dark, often sunburnt complexion, a narrow face with high cheekbones, a straight, thin nose and a full-lipped, sensitive mouth, suggesting weakness. His physique is tall, slender and wiry, and his demeanour is shy, restless, rebellious and a little delicate. All the details are not mentioned for all of the characters, and there are some variations in the color of eyes and hair. Yet in general, the image conforms—with the interesting exception of the frequently mentioned weak, sensual mouth—to photographs of O'Neill taken throughout his lifetime.

The reflection he saw in the stage mirror was a strangely softened portrait of the saturnine, hard, disciplined man he became in his maturity. The theatrical face reveals consistently a softer man, a somewhat sentimentalized dreamer. With the exceptions of Michael Cape and John Loving, the character is young, in his late adolescence or early twenties. He is artistic, a writer, painter or poet, and he holds himself apart from a world that he views as his enemy. He loathes its materialism and seeks to escape it by "belonging" to something beyond life. In this, he reveals a pervasive death-wish suggesting that he will try to avoid undergoing the process of struggle and maturation. Certain of the characters develop positively. John

Loving, for instance, finds his faith, but by and large, the course the character charts through his life is a downward one, leading to the destruction of the bright, adolescent dreams.

Setting Simon Harford momentarily aside, no one of the characters finds a significant sexual fulfillment. Indeed, each one of them turns away from sexual experience. As Dion Anthony makes love to Margaret, he denies life, and he seeks out Cybel for reasons other than her sexuality. Michael Cape hopes for something beyond sexual love, that will prove "a faith in which to relax," and he too refuses a sexual encounter with the prostitute. Richard Miller, who like Cape and Anthony turns away from the whore, is transfixed in innocence in a moment of pre-sexual puppy-love. Stephen Murray refuses Eileen Carmody's love so long as it offers sexual possibility. John Loving's casual adultery produces a convulsion of spirit that rocks his faith. John Brown and Robert Mayo emerge from their minimal sexual encounters filled with hostility toward the women who have caused them to betray their dreams. The self-portrait is oddly antiseptic. None of the characters O'Neill cast in his own image, Dion excepted, reveals his tendency toward dissipation, nor displays his knowledge of life in the lower depths.

Reasons for his imaging of himself as an innocent might be attributed to personal reticence, or to fastidiousness that rejected public confession. It is also true that each of the characters is an image, formed for a specific theatrical occasion, but like any reflection existing without past or future and empty of physical and psychological depth. With this possibility there can be no quarrel. Self-portraits or not, they are creatures of the imagination, and O'Neill cannot be denied the editorial rights and privileges of any author.

With the creation of Edmund Tyrone, however, the conditions change. Edmund is more than an imaginary figure. He is a figure from history and one upon whose truth-to-life an audience has a right to insist. Yet he is cut in the same pattern as the earlier self-portraits and emerges as a curiously two-dimensional reflection, whose past has been bowdlerized and whose negative characteristics are only lightly touched. It cannot be. If Mary and Tyrone and Jamie are "true," then Edmund should be equally so. If the characters in the play are "what the past has made them," then Edmund's past is of grave concern, as are the ambitions and desires that will move him on in the future. The past, however, is not there as it is with the others. The future is never suggested. He remains a participating observer, a little apart, an eavesdropping creature of the imagination. The truth, whatever it was, is at least distorted.

To seek for a reason why O'Neill drew such a suppressed self-portrait is to move toward areas of psychoanalysis that are not relevant here. What-ever the reason, it was not only simple reticence at public self-exposure or a lack of frankness in dealing with some aspects of his own nature in other guises. To counter charges of mere shyness, there is the figure of Simon Harford, whose face is very like that of Edmund Tyrone. Moreover, there are three others, very different characters from the dreaming poet, in whose general aspect something of the essence of O'Neill's theatrical image may be noted: Eben Cabot, Reuben Light and Orin Mannon. Eben's physical characteristics are not described in detail. His hair is dark, he is tall and sinewy, and he has about him a "fierce repressed vitality." Reuben is tall and thin, has the typical large, sensitive eyes and indecisive mouth, but his thick curly hair is red blond, and his jaw is "stubborn." Orin Mannon, whose resemblance to his father and to Adam Brant is marked, is tall and thin and has the acquiline nose, dark complexion, black hair and sensitive mouth of the O'Neill portraits. Each of the four has in him the somewhat feminine weakness and the "touch of the poet" displayed in the routine self-portraits, but there is additionally represented a capacity for sensual experience, a maturity, a masculinity that the dreamers lack. Eben, closest to a dreamer of the four, has a harshness, an animal quality and an eagerness for sexual encounter that is manifested in his encounters with the prostitute, Min, and later with his stepmother. Reuben begins in a condition of adoles-cent weakness, but his nature hardens and in his seduction and murder of Ada, he too reveals his capability for passion. So with Orin and Simon, who emerge more fully, more in three dimensions and with greater strength and masculinity than do any of the easier, sympathetic self-portraits.

The lives of the four are similar, their desires astonishingly special. Each is oedipally in love with his mother. Each is embittered by her loss and feels either that she has betrayed him, or that by seeking to possess her, he has betrayed her. Yet without her he is lost and must in compensation seek a surrogate. Eben, Reuben and Orin, each in revulsion from the attempt to find the mother in another woman, call the surrogate a whore. Thus Eben, when he comes to believe that Abbie has seduced him in order that her child may possess the farm, tells her that he hates her and that she is "a damn trickin' whore!" As he kills Ada, Reuben calls her "Harlot!" and Orin, when Lavinia, who has blossomed and come to resemble her mother, confesses to kissing the Tahitian native, cries out "You—you whore! I'll kill you!" Simon attempts to turn Sara into a whore, and at the same time to use her as a substitute for Deborah who has been lost in her dreams of being a royal whore.

The search for the surrogate mother turns each man toward a condi-tion that is child-like. Reuben, Orin and Simon seek to become children again and to rejoin their mothers in death or in mad dreams. Eben, who in possessing Abbie has felt that he has also possessed his mother, moves toward a final position that is more resolute than the others. Yet midway in the play, the gratification of the child comes to him as well. To be sure, Dion's relations with Cybel have some of the characteristics of the search for the mother in the whore. The great difference between Dion and the others, however, is the degree of sexuality involved in the relationship. Between Dion and Cybel there is no sex, and furthermore there is between them no suggestion of incestuous desire as there is in the other plays.

The dissimilarity between these four characters and the other portraits of the poetic dreamer of which Edmund Tyrone is a culmination is vast. Importantly, the difference is not one of increased revelation, of plunging deeper into the dreamer to reveal more of the man. The difference is really in kind, and it evolves from a difference in subject. Although they wear a face that resembles that of Edmund Tyrone, they are in fact another character, one who conforms closely to the characterization O'Neill drew of his brother in both the Tyrone plays.

In *Long Day's Journey into Night*, Jamie's need for his mother is the central explanation for his despair. His revulsion against her and himself is extreme. It is he who calls Mary a "Hophead" and who marks her final entrance with the "self-defensively sardonic" cry: "The Mad Scene. Enter Ophelia!" He confesses to hating Edmund because "it was your being born that started Mama on dope," and he dates his own dereliction from the day he first "got wise" when he saw her injecting herself with morphine. "Christ," he says, "I'd never dreamed before that any women but whores took dope." What he feels to be his mother's whore-like behavior has left him with no belief. That Mary had appeared to be beating the habit "meant so much," he says. "I'd begun to hope, if she'd beaten the game, I could too." When he realizes that she has defeated his hope, he heads for the local brothel and goes upstairs with the least attractive, and, it is to be assumed, the most maternal of the whores, Fat Violet, who drinks so much and is so overweight that the madam has determined to get rid of her. He summarizes the experience:

> By applying my natural God-given talents in their proper sphere, I shall attain the pinnacle of success! I'll be the lover of the fat woman in Barnum and Bailey's circus! . . . Pah! Imagine me sunk to the fat girl in a hick town hooker shop! . . . But you're right. To hell with repining! Fat Violet's a good kid. Glad I stayed with her. Christian act. Cured her of blues. Hell of a good time. You should have stuck with me, Kid. Taken your

mind off your troubles. What's the use coming home to get the blues over what can't be helped. All over—finished now—not a hope! . . .

> "If I were hanged on the highest hill,
> Mother o' mine, O mother o' mine!
> I know whose love would follow me still"

The maternal whore and the mother whose addiction is a whore's addiction merge in Jamie's befuddled consciousness as the source of his self-disgust and his need.

The Fat Violet episode served in all probability as the basis for a romantic fantasy surrounding that need in *A Moon for the Misbegotten.* Jamie's account of his actions with the whore on the train while he was bringing his mother's body home suggests the same pattern of loss, the same despairing self-destruction as the earlier play did. Not having the mother, he must expend his spirit on the most repulsive facsimile he can find in an orgy of self-defilement. Later, he finds peace with Josie Hogan, the giant woman, who pretends to be a whore, but who is really a virgin, and who in the course of hearing Jamie's confession, holds him pièta-fashion through the long, calm night, as if she were a "virgin who bears a dead child in the night, and the dawn finds her still a virgin." In his drunkenness, Jamie sometimes confuses Josie with the "blonde pig" on the train, but at other times she becomes much more than a substitute for his lost mother: she becomes a mother in truth. As she kisses him, "*There is passion in her kiss but it is a tender, protective maternal passion, which he responds to with an instant grateful yielding.*" Josie, finally, in her double role of mother and whore, can bring to Jamie his mother's forgiveness and blessing. As he sobs himself to sleep on her breast she tells him she forgives him as his mother forgives and loves and understands them both. In his last play, it was fitting that O'Neill should create the woman who could be in reality for his brother what other of his characters—Eben, Reuben, Orin and Simon—had sought with such frenzy.

These four men, although they appear to have Eugene's face, are more nearly to be recognized as portraits of Jamie as the Tyrone plays depicted him. If this is so, three explanations for the transference may be considered. The first is that the oedipal tendencies were in truth Eugene's and that in presenting them on stage, he could not be sufficiently honest to expose himself, and, for this reason, when the character became expressly autobiographical in the Tyrone plays, disguised his need as Jamie's. Against this stands the biographical evidence, especially the story of Jamie's behavior after his mother's death as it is accurately recounted in *A Moon for the*

Misbegotten. Clearly Jamie was possessed of an overt oedipal drive, and the portrait in the Tyrone plays rings true.

A second possibility is that both brothers reacted to the situation in identical ways. Some biographical evidence might support such a conclusion. O'Neill was well known in the brothels of New London and New York. *Strange Interlude* and *The Great God Brown* reveal that he was concerned imaginatively with the symbolism of the whore and the mother that could be found in ancient religious myths and particularly in those associated with Dionysus. Mrs. O'Neill said that on his deathbed her husband reached out and took her hand and said to her, "You are my mamma now." The phrase occurs in other wordings in the plays and could imply that the desire to find the mother in the wife underlay an oedipal necessity of long standing. Macgowan records that O'Neill told him after the interviews with Dr. Hamilton that he was suffering from an oedipus complex, and Louis Sheaffer claims that in his nurse, Sarah Sandy, the young O'Neill found a surrogate mother. Yet no biographer has presented an O'Neill so obsessed with the need for a mother as the four characters, if taken literally as self-portraits, might suggest he was. Sheaffer makes the point that O'Neill, feeling that the other members of his family blamed him for his mother's addiction, stood on the defensive with all three, and held himself alone, very much his own man. As Sheaffer relates it, O'Neill's sexual initiation, a hideously traumatic experience, might well mean that despite his youthful profligacy, there remained in him "a residue of puritanism, of regarding sex as immoral, a result to some extent of his Catholic indoctrination." Sheaffer further suggests that the cult of the Virgin Mary, one that tended to foster "guilt feelings about the flesh," was something O'Neill carried with him from his early days in Catholic schools, and that it was kept alive if not increased in O'Neill by his mother's personality. He writes, "Ella, from all indications was sexually inhibited and lacking in sensuality; her drug addiction clearly signaled a retreat from the responsibilities and obligations of her position, including those as a sex partner." Adequate resolution of the questions is impossible to achieve, but the biographical evidence points toward O'Neill's repression of any aggressive or overt sexual demonstrations toward his mother. On the other hand there is ample evidence that Jamie's life displayed an attraction for his mother openly and continually.

A third alternative may be suggested: that what O'Neill saw and explored at first in self-portraits—through the figures of Eben, Reuben, Orin and Simon—and later, in the Tyrone plays, through Jamie, was both himself *and* Jamie. Or, more specifically, he inspected that part of himself that was in effect Jamie's creation, that to which Jamie referred when he told Edmund, "Hell, you're more than my brother. I made you! You're my Frankenstein!"

The implication of the Frankenstein image is that Jamie was both the creator and destroyer of his brother. Jamie reminds Edmund that it was he who first interested him in reading poetry and he who, because he wanted to write, gave his brother the idea of becoming a writer. By moulding Edmund's tastes and encouraging his talent, Jamie gave himself a kind of creative life. The negative aspect, however, appears as well, as Jamie brags how he introduced his brother to alcohol and to the whores with whom he found release. In the play, speaking in vino veritas, Jamie claims that he dragged Edmund down "to make a bum" of him, and that he did it in full consciousness:

> Or part of me did. A big part. That part that's been dead so long. That hates life. My putting you wise so you'd learn from my mistakes. Believed that myself at times, but it's a fake. Made my mistakes look good. Made getting drunk romantic. Made whores fascinating vampires instead of poor, stupid, diseased slobs they really are. Made fun of work as sucker's game. Never wanted you succeed and make me look even worse by comparison. Wanted you to fail. Always jealous of you. Mama's baby. Papa's pet!

Loving and hating his brother, Jamie has tried to create Edmund in his own image, possessing him in an almost demonic way. In the play, Edmund refuses to pay attention to Jamie's confession, but the Frankenstein image is nowhere denied.

The imagery implies that Jamie was responsible both for Edmund's positive qualities and also for their opposite, the negatives that led him to follow a course of self-destruction. To some extent these polarities exist in all of O'Neill self-portraits, starting with a simple opposition of a poetic man with a crassly materialistic society. Quickly, however, as O'Neill became capable of more complex conceptions of human nature, the creative and self-destructive forces were centered within the hero, as in Stephen Murray and Michael Cape. As yet, however, there was no radical division of personality, but this was to come and it was to be expressed in strange intermingling of personalities.

Between Dion Anthony and William Brown, a fraternal relationship exists. Yet it goes beyond this. Dion assumes Brown's rights when he takes Margaret, but later Brown reverses the relationship and absorbs Dion by wearing his mask. Speaking to the mask of the dead Dion, he talks of how he will assume Dion's role and says, "Then you—the I in you—*I* will live in Margaret." Something of the same closeness may be sensed in Eben's relationship, not to his brothers, but to his father. The two are the "dead spit an' image" of one another, mirrored reflections, bound yet opposite. Again the conception of a man divided into very different, opposed but closely bound beings is in *Mourning Becomes Electra*, where Orin, Ezra and Adam have the same desires and the same face, and yet are locked in a death struggle. The most extreme example is, of course, John and Loving in *Days without End*, where only by an act of exorcism can the negative force be eliminated from the divided soul.

The image shifts, dazzles, puzzles, but the provocative possibility is that O'Neill believed that his brother had done as he claimed, and that part of him *was* Jamie, and, therefore, that Jamie was more than his brother, was somehow an image of himself, an image that was a hostile double, bent on his destruction, a form of *doppelgänger*.

The myth of the demonic double is perhaps more a literary affectation than a reality in men's minds. Despite many early anticipations of the idea, the legend was given form in early nineteenth-century Gothic thrillers like *Frankenstein*. It persisted, however, in a not entirely literary form. In a brief, seminal treatise, *The Double*, Otto Rank has shown that the legend can become an actuality in the neurotic fantasies of disturbed personalities. In legend, the double emerges from a mirror or shadow and detaches itself from the man who gave it form. Henceforth, the man is without reflection. Instead the double moves through life in a mysterious course parallel to his progenitor and at each crucial turn steps between the man and his achievement. The double accepts his triumphs, steals the love he has sought and in the end destroys him.

In anthropological investigation and in areas of psychoanalytic study the double, as Rank presents it, is a product of paranoid fantasy, involving fear of inexplicable and hostile pursuit. Yet Rank points out that in addition to paranoia another syndrome appears:

> We know that the person of the pursuer frequently represents the father or his substitute (brother, teacher, etc.), and we also find in our material that the double is often identified with the brother. It is clearest in Musset [in "December Night"] but also appears in Hoffman . . . , Poe, Dostoevsky, and others. The appearance for the most part is as a twin and reminds us of the legend of the womanish Narcissus, for Narcissus thinks that he sees in his image his sister, who resembles him in every respect.

That those writers who preferred the theme of the double also had to contend with the male sibling complex follows from the not infrequent treatment of fraternal rivalry in their other works.

Rank continues to discuss this fraternal rivalry toward the hated competitor in the love for the mother and ultimately the death wish of the subject. He adds, "The most prominent symptom of the forms which the double takes is a powerful consciousness of guilt which forces the hero no longer to accept the responsibility for certain actions of his ego, but to place it upon another ego, a double, who is either personified by the devil himself or is created by making a diabolical pact." He also suggests that slaying of the double, "through which the hero seeks to protect himself permanently from the pursuits of his self, is really a suicidal act."

In O'Neill's plays, the double, divested of its Gothic horror, and therefore without the suggestions of paranoia, appears continually: in *Days without End*, in the deep divisions of personality of many of the characters in *Strange Interlude* and the extant cycle plays, in *Ah, Wilderness!*, where the division of each member of O'Neill's family into two characters exorcises guilt, in Orin Mannon's sense that having killed Adam Brant he has killed himself—the list can be multiplied. What is of immediate interest, however, is that while the plays correspond with startling exactitude to much of Rank's analysis, O'Neill creates a significant variation on the pattern. The variation is suggested in *Beyond the Horizon*. Andrew has taken Robert's life and despoiled it, and in the context he may well be thought of as the double. But it is equally true that Robert has taken Ruth from Andrew and spoiled his brother's life. From another point of view, Robert might well be considered Andrew's double. In *The Great God Brown*, Billy steals Dion's talent and takes his wife by assuming his appearance. Clearly this is the way of the double, but so is Dion's macabre mockery of Billy and his theft of Margaret in the beginning of the play. As with Robert and Andrew, as with the doubles in the Mannon family, which is the self? Which the double? In O'Neill's plays it is not entirely evident that the self, in all instances a self-portrait, has sufficiently strong identity to make clear which of the "brothers" is the reflected image of the other.

A possible explanation lies in Jamie's image of Frankenstein. If it is true that O'Neill, however unconsciously, felt himself to be Jamie's creation and in particular viewed his own negative tendencies as implantations Jamie had made, it may be argued that he drew the self-portraits, both those presenting a corrupted, poetic innocent and those of the sensual, even destructive man, as a way of sorting out what lay within him. To understand

Jamie was not difficult, as *Long Day's Journey into Night* attests, but to understand what Jamie had done to Eugene may have been nearly impossible. Was it that Jamie had stolen Eugene's life? Or was it that Jamie was Eugene's Loving? If Eugene was Jamie's Frankenstein, what was Eugene's truth? O'Neill's growing interest in the God-denying materialist, first seen in *Marco Millions* and continuing through the cycle, appears to reflect his growing need to analyze the uncreative qualities within himself. Searching in mirrors to discover whether anyone is there is to look for the double within. In the end it was the essence of Jamie in himself that became of concern and that may have led Eugene to draw Jamie as Eben, Reuben, Orin and Simon, as a way of looking at Jamie when Jamie became Eugene. It was an instinctive way of separating the elements within to discover what Eugene was and what it meant to be Jamie's Frankenstein.

This cannot be the truth of it. O'Neill was an artist, not a do-it-yourself psychoanalyst. Yet some implications of the suggestion may shed light on O'Neill's career as a playwright. After 1922, the year of his mother's death, with the single exception of his adaptation of *The Ancient Mariner*, all the extant plays reveal some direct autobiography. Far from inventing dramatic fictions to please and move his audiences, O'Neill's imagination turned to the creation of narrative masks for a central situation among four people he obsessively sought to understand. He did not dramatize the full situation all of the time, but aspects of it are to be found in the central focus of thirty-five of the plays. Edmund Tyrone, who stumbles in from the fog where he has walked as if he were "a ghost belonging to the fog," returns from the dead to tell his father of his vision of belonging to a life force. So Lazarus was resurrected to speak of the life force, and Hickey, coming from a murder, comatose, as if he were dead, returns to Hope's to preach a vision. The concern of Nina's three men for her welfare reflects the care of the three male Tyrones for Mary's health. The image of the poet destroyed by the materialist has multiple recurrences, and characters return: the mother who is a betrayer of her children and who resents being the object of their need; brothers bound in opposition; wives who persecute their husbands; fathers and children fixed in a pattern of love and hate; the maternal whore to whom men turn for surcease; men and women who feed on dreams. The list is long, but it evolves from a single, central source, the action of *Long Day's Journey into Night*, in which O'Neill's whole creative life centered. He had to write the play; literally, he lived to write it.

In the play's dedication, O'Neill thanks his wife for giving him "the faith in love that enabled me to face my dead at last and write this play— write it with deep pity and understanding and forgiveness for *all* the four haunted Tyrones." Pity, understanding and forgiveness surely are there for three of them, but for Edmund the understanding, the pity and perhaps the forgiveness is less pervasive. Edmund is only a slightly more mature version of the sentimental rebel O'Neill created in Richard Miller. Except in such episodes as his reaction to his father's attempt to put him into a cheap sanatorium, his responses to his family are not specifically defined. He repeatedly avoids conflict, refuses to face issues, remains neutral and a little passive. Partly the blandness may be because Jamie is now on stage in his own person, and much that O'Neill had previously explored of Jamie in himself is now, as it were, returned to its source. About Jamie, as about his mother and father, O'Neill, the playwright, is totally perceptive. Their relationships to one another as well as to Edmund are strongly and clearly defined. His to them are not. Perhaps, if *Long Day's Journey into Night* may be called a "dream play," an explanation might lie in the fact that Edmund is the dreamer's dream of himself. He moves like a dream's protagonist in wonder and dread, but is uncommitted to the dream's occurrences. Commitment, finally, belongs to the dreamer and not the dream. The play is O'Neill's last mirror, the last time he would look to see if he was "there." In itself, the image of the young, gentle, unhappy man he saw proved nothing, but having gone through the door in the mind to the fogbound room in the past, he perhaps understood himself as his figure was illuminated by the pain and concern of those about him. In the agony of the others, it is possible, the playwright's identity was at last to be found.

Significant Form:
Long Day's Journey into Night

Jean Chothia

Both *The Iceman Cometh* and *Long Day's Journey into Night* are set in 1912, and present a group of people isolated together from the world. But they are antithetical in several ways. One takes place in a New York City bar, the other in a family home in a New England small town. In the one play, a large group of men of widely different backgrounds are met in a society constructed by them to meet their needs and O'Neill explores their relationship to each other and to that society, letting us glimpse more intimate personal relationships through the eyes of only one of the participants. In the other play, the scale of the action is narrowed to just such intimate relationships. The four characters belong to a nuclear family and O'Neill explores the nature of their bondage to it and to each other. For all its breadth, *The Iceman Cometh* is the less complex of the two plays in construction and emotional effect. The images it projects disturb the audience and make them sharply aware of contradictions normally thrust aside in the activity of daily living. Those of *Long Day's Journey into Night* take the audience into their very selves. In both plays, the audience are made conscious that chaos and isolation lie threateningly behind the action but, whereas in *The Iceman Cometh* the character who perceives this most fully is continually moved to the periphery of the action, all four characters in *Long Day's Journey into Night* move steadily closer to articulation of such knowledge.

The multiplicity of *The Iceman Cometh*, the impression we have of

From *Forging a Language: A Study of the Plays of Eugene O'Neill.* © 1979 by Cambridge University Press.

there being many changes and happenings to take into account, the theatrical zest of the piece, derive from the astonishing range of character pro-
jected. In *Long Day's Journey into Night*, there are four major characters,
where in the earlier play there were seventeen. Whatever variety or intensity, sadness or humour the play has must come from the dialogue and
gesture of these four. My purpose [here] is to consider how it does so.

The language offers an immediate measure of the change in focus
between *The Iceman Cometh* and *Long Day's Journey into Night*. The bold
range of national and class dialect of the earlier play is not found in the
later, where all four characters speak Standard American English. Their
speech is no less clearly differentiated than in the earlier play but the process
of recognition here is a slower one. The audience gradually becomes
attuned, through shifts in the syntactic and lexical arrangement of the dialogue and through recurrent topics of conversation, to the various registers
which exist within the speech of each character. The smaller number of
characters and the more gradual method of projecting them, allow O'Neill
to probe behind the idiosyncratic surface and explore the varying and even
conflicting elements of individual identity. The method is similar to that
used in presenting Larry Slade but is developed in a more intensive way.
Whereas the old anarchist sat alone at the edge of the stage, the characters
here are all fully embroiled in the action and continually interact with each
other. When new information causes us to alter our assumptions about a
character then our idea of his relationship with each of the other characters
is altered, too.

The conventions associated with drama help to shape the audience's
acceptance of the illusion of the reality of the stage world. Compared with
people in life, the characters of *The Iceman Cometh* are caricatures and yet,
as we have seen, they have an extraordinary vitality during the play. In his
essay on Tourneur, Eliot pointed out the necessity of characters being "real
in relation to each other" if the conventions are to operate and said:

> [Tourneur's characters] may be distortions, grotesques, almost
> childish caricatures of humanity, but they are all distorted to
> scale. Hence the whole action, from their appearance to their
> ending, "no common action" indeed, has its own self-subsistent
> reality.
>
> (*Elizabethan Dramatists*)

Having noted the importance of internal consistency, we must also ac-
knowledge that there are plays whose action and emotion seem more

searingly close to ourselves than is usual, whose characters, as Eliot says elsewhere of Shakespeare's figures, "represent a more complex tissue of feelings and desires as well as a more supple, a more susceptible temperament" than we normally find in plays. In the common shorthand, such figures are labelled "fully rounded" or "three dimensional". But whilst such characters have been readily enough identified, there have been few attempts to discover how they are created in the dialogue.

Many commentators, attributing the roundedness of the characters of *Long Day's Journey into Night* to the autobiographical origins of the play, have been concerned to describe O'Neill's private relationships in the period in which the play is set. But this is to slide away from the crucial questions about how the play works, since autobiographical writing is not, *per se*, binding on its audience. Although the personal nature of the material may well quicken the writer's imagination, it can only speak to the audience when it has been shaped by that imagination into an artistic form with its own unity, apart from the life.

If the play is an emotionally harrowing experience, it is so because of the stage characters and the stage action. However lifelike they seem, characters have their existence only in relation to the stage action, and exist in their particular form because of the way the writer has selected and organized words and gestures. The dramatist writes dialogue, not speech, and presents not the O'Neills, who are people, but the Tyrones, who are characters.

In the wake of the various psychological and sociological descriptions of personality of the last hundred years, have come a succession of attacks on the idea of richly delineated, autonomous characters in fiction by writers who claim that these belie reality with their false coherence. In the preface to *Lady Julie*, in one of the earliest of such statements, Strindberg argued that if the dramatist is to reveal ourselves to ourselves he must do so through figures that are characterless since, far from being the self-consistent wholes generally portrayed on the stage, people are unpredictable, "vacillating," "riven asunder." His own characters he described as being:

> conglomerations from past and present stages of civilization; they are excerpts from books and newspapers, scraps of humanity, pieces torn from festive garments which have become rags—just as the soul itself is a piece of patchwork. Besides this, I have provided a little evolutionary history in making the weaker repeat phrases stolen from the stronger, and in making

my souls borrow "ideas"—suggestions, as they are called, from one another.

(trans. C. D. Locoćk, *International Modern Plays* [Everyman])

But such is the force of the convention that we assimilate and order the fragmentary information and create for ourselves a clear idea of the three individuals, Julie, Jean and Kristen, who appear on the stage. The audience draws from the text the kind of characterization that the pattern of set, plot and coherent dialogue leads it to expect. It is only when Strindberg robs us of these expectations by positing the play as a dream and not a mimesis of life, in the Chamber plays and *To Damascus*, that the audience finds itself unable to naturalize the text in this way.

O'Neill seems to have shared Strindberg's theory of human personality but, in writing the play, takes the audience's ordering impulse as his starting point. He develops an idiosyncratic language pattern for each character, thus differentiating them and giving each an identity. He then proceeds to vary and occasionally break these patterns so that each speaks with several different and even conflicting voices. Each appears many-faceted, an unpredictable amalgam and yet, at any given moment, still himself, distinct from any other figure on the stage.

The method of *Long Day's Journey into Night*, like that of *The Iceman Cometh* was prefigured in a less complex way in the early plays. As we saw [earlier], Jim Harris's low-colloquial speech, in *All God's Chillun Got Wings*, was modified towards Standard by stages throughout the play. At the realistic level, his growing articulacy indicated his educational progress and marked the passing of time whilst, at the symbolic level, it signalled his spiritual growth. In *Desire under the Elms*, O'Neill attempted something rather more complicated. Ephraim's New England low-colloquial was coloured by an idiosyncratic use of biblical vocabulary and syntax which became more evident when he was roused by anger or lust. Filtered into the speech of other characters, particularly at moments when they sought to defy Ephraim, such religious language revealed the influence of the old man on them. So, James Tyrone's speech mode in *Long Day's Journey into Night* varies according to his emotional state and, at times, both sons echo his manner. Mary Tyrone's utterance is closer to the model of Jim Harris in that her speech changes under the influence of the drug she takes and is actually different from act to act. Changes in her speech serve to mark the passage of time too although, here, the movement is not from present to future, but from present to remembered past. Jamie uses two distinct and conflicting registers, one of which is usually consciously adopted but sometimes seems to take demonic possession, whilst Edmund, still a young man with several paths open to him, has a range of voices some directly imitative of Jamie or of the writers he admires, but none so distinct as those of the other members of the family. . . .

One of the more firmly fixed dramatic conventions is that there should be a hero, a central figure. Much of the emotional intensity of this play derives from O'Neill's deliberate breaking of the convention. The audience's impulse to identify with one character is continually satisfied and then frustrated. At any given moment, one of the four dominates the action revealing his thought in such a way that our sympathy is engaged but, immediately, his words and gestures alienate that sympathy and his place is taken by another. The resulting tension binds the audience to the action by insisting that they hold the claims of all four characters in mind and delay judgement on what they see. Even as one figure expresses his spiritual isolation, we find ourselves relating his words to each of the other three and, by extension, to all human experience. The relationship between the four characters, from which none can wholly separate himself, is as much O'Neill's subject as is the quest of each for individual meaning. As the play proceeds, we recognize that each character is both supported and crippled by the relationship and that these elements are tightly enmeshed. O'Neill uses particular linguistic devices to create what might be called a "family rhythm." These are responsible for much of the surface variety of the play and also for its underlying coherence, since they permeate the action, seeming to root the characters together in their shared past.

Most obviously, but nevertheless importantly for the tone of the play, the characters address each other familiarly. They tease each other about little personal matters, snoring, reducing, digesting. They laugh at the same jokes. The Shaughnessy joke, for example, told by Edmund in act 1, is humorous in itself, but is used by O'Neill as a surface event behind whose cover he can demonstrate the patterns of grievance and affection which coexist between the characters. The family comes together to share the joke but breaks apart immediately when father turns the laughter into an attack on son, and the story itself is repeatedly interrupted by the tangential comments of the listeners which reveal their private attitudes and indicate their habitual positions. Quarrels, too, flair out of nothing and are quickly deflated, allegiances shift and each character puts in his word in a manner possible only amongst people with a history of such interactions. O'Neill is confronting the audience with the pattern of its own familiar conversations and asking them to leap its gaps and understand its shared assumptions. Something of this can be seen in a fairly lighthearted exchange early in act 1: Edmund breaks into a conversation about other matters with a reference back to Mary's earlier complaint about Tyrone's snoring:

> EDMUND. I'll back you up about Papa's snoring. Gosh, what a racket!
> JAMIE. I heard him, too. (*He quotes, putting on a ham-actor manner.*) "The Moor, I know his trumpet." (*His mother and brother laugh.*)
> TYRONE (*scathingly*). If it takes my snoring to make you remember Shakespeare instead of the dope sheet on the ponies, I hope I'll keep on with it.
> MARY. Now, James! You mustn't be so touchy. (*Jamie shrugs his shoulders and sits down in the chair on her right.*)
> EDMUND (*irritably*). Yes, for Pete's sake, Papa! The first thing after breakfast! Give it a rest, can't you? (*He slumps down in the chair at left of table next to his brother. His father ignores him.*)
> MARY (*reprovingly*). Your father wasn't finding fault with you. You don't have to always take Jamie's part. You'd think you were the one ten years older.

Jamie caps Edmund's words, Edmund Mary's and the dialogue flows quickly from statement to reaction, the alternation of second and first person pronouns helping the movement of the sequence. Each utterance endorses, contradicts or extends the preceding one. The startling personal attack by father on son and the speed with which the other two characters intervene, suggest that there is knowledge involved which predates the play and alert us to meanings beyond the common core of the words spoken. Using the predisposition of the audience to seek out significance, O'Neill embeds his exposition of situation and character into the flow of the dialogue. There is no narration in this play of the kind spoken by Larry to Parritt at the opening of *The Iceman Cometh*. There are only fragments which the audience must piece together. The use, here, of the continuous form of the verb, and of adverbs of time, such as Mary's "always," suggest that we are witnessing a habitual response, and this impression will be reinforced when these two features recur, as they frequently do, in expressions of irritation between the characters ("Papa, if you're starting that stuff again!"; "You always imagine things"; "I could see that line coming! God, how many thousand times"). We gather specific information, too, about Jamie's wastrel life, the relative ages of the two brothers, Tyrone's respect for Shakespeare, and we can deduce that both brothers must have been awake during the night although the significance of this will only become apparent with the accumulation of several such hints. Similarly, we hear a comic distortion of a quotation and an irritable response to it—the first piece of a pattern which will be elaborated during the play.

The open method of exposition is particularly appropriate to this play. What the audience learns about the past might be detailed, but it can never be fixed because it is refracted through the consciousness of one or other of the characters and, far from endorsing any one account, O'Neill lets each contradict the others. Whilst some details are allowed to seem fairly stable, other topics—homes, doctors, the electric light, the fog, alcohol—are raised, dropped and taken up again by each character, each new reference modifying the audience's viewpoint until, by the end of the play, each topic is fraught with suggestion. To take one small example: we have seen that there are numerous references to the electric light which gradually becomes a symbol of Tyrone's financial anxiety, the cause of much of the family suffering and bitterness. When Jamie enters drunk in act 4 we seem to be being presented with the traditional stage comedy of the drunken man. All the elements are here, the slurred speech and lurching movement; the recourse to tired, moralistic proverbs and the attribution of human intentions to the objects with which he collides, but there is also a succession of references in word and gesture to fog and clarity, darkness and light ("Ought to be a lighthouse out there"; "What the hell is this, the morgue?"; "Lesh have some light on sibject"; "Ford o' Kabul river in the dark! . . ."; "Can't expect us to live in the Black Hole of Calcutta") which not only communicates Jamie's hostility to his absent father but recalls the long scene between Edmund and Tyrone and contributes to the symbolic undercurrent of the play.

We catch echoes of one character's speech in that of another. The speech of both Tyrone and Mary has an Irish shape much like that of Larry Slade which appears most noticeably when they tease each other affectionately or dream of the past. This helps to suggest the warmth of their feeling at such moments and also marks the experiential gap between parent and child. The brogue itself is not used but a cluster of references makes the idea of Ireland into a signal of the insecurity of the uprooted man. The American-born sons can cut deep with scornful references to the ancient homeland. Tyrone's tale of self-help follows the classical American immigrant pattern of rejection of origins coupled with staunch loyalty to them. He has rid himself of his brogue but has surrounded himself with his own tribe in the shape of tenant, housemaid, drinking companions. Elsewhere, shared language can mark the deep, unacknowledged bond between parent and child. Edmund's speech in act 4 which begins, "The fog was where I wanted to be," is a moving example of this. Although he, as much as the others, has resented his mother's retreat into herself, Edmund, here, not only echoes her longing to withdraw but, in doing so, takes over the words which recur in her speech and in descriptions of her: "fog," "alone," "lost," "hide" and "ghost." Soon after this, Jamie comments drunkenly on his own quotation of Wilde's "The Harlot's House," saying, "Not strictly accurate. If my love was with me I didn't notice it. She must have been a ghost." The uncanny impression of Mary's presence, created by the collocation in Edmund's speech of words normally associated with her, is likely to make the audience sensitive to the word "ghost" when it occurs again in Jamie's speech. Without making anything explicit, O'Neill allows the audience to perceive the unconscious irony of Jamie's words and to recognize the part his relationship with his mother has played in warping his life. We might contrast, here, the explicitness of the Freudian statements O'Neill used in the middle plays, particularly *Strange Interlude* and *Mourning Becomes Electra*, about the relationships between parents and children. By using associations established in the earlier scenes of the play as the material for the dramatic metaphors of the later scenes, the dramatist binds the play into a whole.

Denials and barriers of silence occur frequently. They are as telling as the shared language in revealing what the characters have in common and, as they accumulate, we become aware of their thematic significance. Certain truths are avoided by the Tyrones as firmly as others were in Hope's bar. Things are implied but not stated, a topic is suddenly changed, a speaker falls silent in mid-sentence and the listener forbears to comment. During the first act, for example, we observe the men's concern for Mary, we hear her demands that they trust her and their eager reassurances and we also piece together a grimly comic picture of all three men simulating sleep on the night before the action of the play whilst listening intently to Mary's restless moving about. When any of the men attempts to discuss this the others deny having been conscious of anything extraordinary. The audience's curiosity is aroused. In the second act, the anxiety and shirked confidences of the men are recalled, just before Mary's entrance, in the pause which occurs during this brief exchange:

EDMUND. She didn't get much sleep last night.
JAMIE. I know she didn't. (*A pause. The brothers avoid looking at each other.*)
EDMUND. That damned foghorn kept me awake, too.

The admissions which flood into such silences are more marked because they are spoken only in the minds of the audience. They are ominous because they draw attention to but do not solve the mystery already sensed. Euphemisms are used in the play, with similar effect. Tyrone refers to the drug as "the poison," "her curse," and the other characters avoid naming it. All use the euphemism "summer cold" to disguise their fear of Edmund's illness from themselves and each other. If, in his anxiety, one character forgets the tacit agreement, the others quickly remind him and the pattern of reticence and uneasy collusion is reinforced. For example:

> MARY. You mustn't mind Edmund, James. Remember he isn't well. (*Edmund can be heard coughing as he goes upstairs.*) (*She adds nervously.*) *A summer cold* makes anyone *irritable.*
>
> JAMIE (*genuinely concerned*). It's not just a cold he's got. The Kid is damned sick. (*His father gives him a sharp warning look but he doesn't see it.*)
>
> MARY (*turns on him resentfully*). Why do you say that? It is *just a cold!* Anyone can tell that! You always imagine things!
>
> TYRONE (*with another warning glance at Jamie—easily*). All Jamie meant was Edmund might have *a touch of something else*, too, which makes his cold worse.
>
> JAMIE. Sure, Mama. *That's all* I meant.
>
> TYRONE. Doctor Hardy thinks it might be *a bit of* malarial fever he caught when he was in the tropics. If it is, quinine will soon cure it.

Such passages help to show the guilt and panic underlying the relationship. The soothing words, which infiltrate the speech of all the characters, as my italicizing in the extract demonstrates, represent a shrinking from the deeper reassurances and admissions for which all long. The euphemisms make us sensitive to the family's private taboos, and it is the effect of a taboo being broken as much as the sudden coarse slang which makes Jamie's bitter attacks on Mary so shocking, or Edmund's cry, "Mama, it isn't a summer cold! I've got consumption," so piercing and Mary's refusal to respond so final.

Throughout the play such denials occur, shifting attention from facts and events to their emotional effect, and infiltrating our consciousness with the looming despair of the Tyrones. We are made painfully aware that the time will never be ripe, that opportunities will always be missed, because O'Neill juxtaposes some of the cruellest denials with moments of brief sympathy, frustrating the expectations of change which are beginning to be shaped. So, in act 1, Jamie and Tyrone break apart with mutual recriminations after their brief understanding. And, when one character tries to break through to another by crying out an appeal, the other retreats in confusion or resentment, as Tyrone does from Mary in act 2 and she from him in the following act. Such withdrawal, as we have seen, becomes a dominant pattern in Mary's speech.

A similar pattern of accretion underlies our impression that the relationship also has its positive aspect. This is most immediately apparent in the confessions of act 4, in which, one after another, each character reveals his trust by attempting to expose his deepest thought. But it is apparent too in much slighter devices. Tyrone, for example, usually avoids Jamie's Christian name. This emphasizes his resentment much as did Larry Slade's avoidance of Parritt's name in *The Iceman Cometh*. But here the pattern is occasionally and significantly broken. In the early part of the play, Tyrone uses the name when there is brief but unambiguous sympathy between the two men, when they discuss Mary or worry about Edmund's sickness. Each expression of affection, although minimal in itself, is strengthened by being linked with others through the recurrent use of the name. The current of feeling so created is a small but persistent one, so that when we hear the name being used by Tyrone in his final utterance, "Pass me that bottle Jamie. And stop reciting that damned morbid poetry. I won't have it in my house," ambiguity creeps in and the audience are reminded of the underlying affection as well as of the habitual irritation. O'Neill's originality, indeed, derives from his capacity to make both the closeness and the resentment within a whole web of relationships—between parent and child, husband and wife, brother and brother—apparent, by intertwining the negative and positive elements. In this, his material differs from Strindberg's in *The Father* and *The Dance of Death*, with which his plays have often been compared, and from Edward Albee's, in *Who's Afraid of Virginia Woolf?*, which was probably influenced by O'Neill. Perhaps of all the forerunners, only Ibsen creates quite the same kind of tension: in the relationship of the two sisters in *John Gabriel Borkman*, for example.

Our sense of the necessity of the family unit to each member, despite all the horrors it holds for them, is established in part by the image we are given of the Tyrones keeping face before the outside world and revealing their fragmented, uncertain selves only to each other. When Tyrone, in act 3, quiets Mary with the words, "Hush now! Here comes Cathleen. You don't want her to see you crying," he bears witness to the existence of an intimacy which does allow her to cry before him. O'Neill presents the difference dramatically by introducing the fifth character, Cathleen. She represents on stage the world beyond the walls of the house. When she is present, and it is only in the central acts, not in the concentrated final section of the play, nor in any of the tauter sequences, the audience briefly see the characters as they would present themselves to the outside world, the world of the pub and the club and the theatre, the whorehouse and the small town. Cathleen is not developed in the way the other characters are, nor is she given the Dickensian individuality of Hope's roomers. Her speech is marked by complacent generalization ("Everybody healthy snores," "It's a good man's failing," "He's a fine gentleman and you're a lucky woman,") and stage-Irish dialect ("Sure, didn't it kill an uncle of mine in the old country," "I'd think you'd a drop taken,"). Her words rarely offer more than their surface meaning and her utterances are short, except when O'Neill needs a contrast with Mary's words when the other three Tyrones are off-stage. Then, he is able to emphasize the seriousness and strangely distant innocence of the mistress's words by means of a painfully humorous contrast with Cathleen's vacuous chatter. A brief extract will demonstrate the effect:

CATHLEEN. Give him half a chance and he's pinching me on the leg or you-know-where — asking your pardon, Ma'am, but it's true.

MARY (*dreamily*). It wasn't the fog I minded, Cathleen. I really love fog.

CATHLEEN. They say it's good for the complexion.

MARY. It hides you from the world and the world from you. You feel that everything has changed, and nothing is what it seemed to be. No one can find or touch you any more.

CATHLEEN. I wouldn't care so much if Smythe was a fine, handsome man like some chauffeurs I've seen—I mean, if it was all in fun, for I'm a decent girl. But for a shriveled runt like Smythe —! I've told him.

Cathleen is, in essence, the conventional comic servant of the nineteenth-century theatre. Because conventional, she is neutral and, so, acceptable as a minor character. She has not sufficient intrinsic interest to intrude on our impression of the family's isolation and, by the same token, can serve as the mirror in which the public face of each is reflected. In her eye, the sons are carefree men about town, Tyrone a good husband and generous gentleman, Mary a considerate mistress and loving mother. The audience is made conscious of the contrast between ordered image and confused reality, without any of the clumsy paraphernalia of masks and scenic devices which were so distracting in the middle plays.

Quotation is a major structural element in *Long Day's Journey into Night*, *A Touch of the Poet* and *A Moon for the Misbegotten*. In the early plays, there were echoes and half-quotations from other writers, the implications of which were often inappropriate to O'Neill's meaning. I suggested [elsewhere] that these were often unconscious intrusions but that when O'Neill wrote *Ah, Wilderness!* he had become sufficiently self-aware to use his feeling for particular literary works as a key element in characterizing the hero of the play. As with O'Neill's other experiments, when the use of quotation appears in the later plays, it is developed with greater complexity.

Three of the characters quote frequently in *Long Day's Journey into Night*. Their choice of writer and the way in which his words are used show the individual minds engaging with life. All three Tyrone men quote from Shakespeare. Tyrone's quotations seem spontaneous because he interrupts himself to utter them:

> There's nothing wrong with life. It's we who—(*He quotes.*)
> "The fault, dear Brutus, is not in our stars, but in ourselves that
> we are underlings."

The old actor rejoices in the very sound and shape of words and, fittingly, his quotations are all from famous speeches in better-known plays—*Julius Caesar, King Lear, The Tempest* (twice). His Shakespeare is the creator, par excellence, of aphorisms and, as such, is recommended: "You'll find it nobly said in Shakespeare"; "You'll find everything you're trying to say in him—as you'll find everything else worth saying," and, in exasperation, "That damned library of yours . . . When I've *three* good sets of Shakespeare you could read." In Tyrone, O'Neill presents the enigma of the man for whom issues must be clear cut and who, despite his own experience, accepts that the universe has a fixed moral law. The quotation enables the dramatist to do this without didacticism. The cruelty of Tyrone's position is brought sharply before us in act 4 when we realize that the writer with whom we have come to associate him is the symbol of the youthful dream that was betrayed and not of the lifetime's work. Indeed, no-one in the family quotes from the "god-damned play" which is not even graced with a name. The only direct reference to any melodrama is Jamie's laboured Old Gaspard joke, and the linking of that with *The Bells* is inaccurate.

Like the attitudes to Ireland, quotation is a means of projecting the father-son relationship. Tyrone quotes Shakespeare straight. His sons deliberately distort although, in much the same way as in *Desire under the Elms*, O'Neill can quietly demonstrate the influence of the old man on the young rebels through the very fact of their familiarity with Shakespeare and the relish with which they quote. Edmund's distortion of Shakespeare is gauche, as we have seen. Jamie's is impressive. He quotes stage directions and asides and, when he quotes from the text itself, he has spied out another meaning for the accurately quoted words. Early in the play his jokes are mild; Othello's trumpet, for example, stands for Tyrone's snoring; but they darken as the play proceeds, culminating in the terrifying flippancy imposed on the normally neutral stage direction, "The mad scene. Enter Ophelia" with which Jamie breaks the silence at Mary's final entrance. The audience must accommodate both the inhumanity of the distortion and the haunting aptness. For the association Jamie makes brings with it a strange, unspoken resonance, best indicated through this description of Ophelia's speech given by the gentleman in Shakespeare's play:

> her speech is nothing,
> Yet the unshaped use of it doth move,
> The hearers to collection; they aim at it,
> And botch the words up fit to their own thoughts;
> Which, as her winks, and nods, and gestures yield them,
> Indeed would make one think there might be thought,
> Though nothing sure, yet much unhappily.
>
> (*Hamlet* 4.5)

The second current of quotation—of *fin de siècle* poetry—is not shared by Tyrone, which in itself is revealing. More subtly, the literary consciousness of the two brothers, though similar, does not entirely coincide. O'Neill uses the difference to show the younger supplanting the elder. Jamie, we are told, wanted to become a writer but Edmund has actually become one, however flawed. The difference is made real in Jamie's only direct personal attack on his brother, which is couched in literary terms:

> Your poetry isn't very cheery. Nor the stuff you read and claim
> you admire. (*He indicates the smart bookcase at rear.*) Your pet
> with the unpronounceable name, for example.
> EDMUND. Nietzsche. You don't know what you're talking about.
> You haven't read him.
> JAMIE. Enough to know it's a lot of bunk!

It is one of the rare instances when Edmund's words are stronger than his brother's, and it prepares the audience for Jamie's subsequent boast and Edmund's calm acceptance of it:

> And who steered you onto reading poetry first? Swinburne, for example? I did! And because I once wanted to write, I planted it in your mind that someday you'd write! Hell, you're more than my brother. I made you! You're my Frankenstein!
>
> EDMUND. All right, I'm your Frankenstein. So let's have a drink. (*He laughs.*) You crazy nut.

It prepares the audience, too, for the terrible warning that follows. The areas of overlap in the brothers' literary consciousness are used as effectively. Jamie quotes self-indulgently, identifying himself with the poet's persona in justification of his wastrel life. But for all their statements about futility, the writers he quotes did set down their thoughts for publication, did image deeds in words, whereas even Jamie's words are borrowed. The audience's response to both the poetry and the man who quotes it is made more ambivalent by Edmund, who seems to use other men's words to stimulate his own. He quotes Dowson's "Days of Wine and Roses" before exploring the experience of his walk in the fog and Baudelaire's "Epilogue," as an introduction to his description of Jamie. We might say that whereas Jamie adopts the role implied by the poetry, Edmund uses it to seek out and comprehend his own experience of the world. Jamie, who takes over the attitude of these poems most completely, is most damaged by the family situation; Edmund, whose response is more ambiguous, seems to have some beliefs which reach beyond the private turmoil and Tyrone, who most determinedly avoids looking closely at his situation, dismisses these poets angrily, as "morbid" purveyors of "filth, despair and pessimism" but is the one who makes their thematic relevance apparent when he says, in unthinking fury, "Don't compare [Shakespeare] with the pack you've got there. . . . Your dirty Zola! And your Dante Gabriel Rossetti who was a dope fiend. (*He starts and looks guilty.*)" The quotation thus helps to make even the very individual afflictions of this family signify a more general pattern of human suffering and mischance.

George Steiner has written of O'Neill's use of quotation:

> Interspersed in the sodden morass of *Long Day's Journey into Night* there are passages from Swinburne. The lines are flamboyant, romantic verbiage. They are meant to show up the adolescent

inadequacies of those who recite them. But, in fact, when the play is performed, the contrary occurs. The energy and glitter of Swinburne's language burn a hole in the surrounding fabric. They elevate the action above its paltry level and instead of showing up the character show up the playwright. Modern writers rarely quote their authors with impunity.

(*Language and Silence* [Penguin edition])

Although, as we have seen, the role of quotation is rather more complex in this play than Steiner suggests, he is half-way towards the truth. Prose cannot speak to the auditory imagination in quite the way that verse does, lingering in the mind when no longer heard, and O'Neill needed this quality of sound, particularly towards the end of the play. In *Moon of the Carribbees*, O'Neill used the sound of a haunting creole lament; in *The Emperor Jones*, the beat of African drums; in *Dynamo*, the hum of the electric generator, and he wrote to the Theatre Guild directors before the production of *Dynamo*, stressing the importance to him of sound in the theatre and saying, "It must be realized that these are not incidental noises but significant dramatic overtones that are an integral part of the composition in the theatre which is the whole play." The foghorn, which sounds during the last act of *Long Day's Journey into Night*, is a sound effect of this kind but the important sound pattern is, appropriately in this play in which language is so deftly structured, a verbal one. The quotations O'Neill uses are unusually melodious and the actors are directed to deliver them sonorously. Swinburne's words do burn and nowhere more so than in the final sequence of the play, which is the one Steiner seems to have had in mind. Here, three stanzas of Swinburne's poem "A Leave-taking" are interwoven with the dialogue of the play. What Steiner does not admit is that the words burn *because* of the context O'Neill has created for them. A comment of Eliot's about the poet is enlightening. "Swinburne's words," he writes, "are all suggestion and no denotation; if they suggest nothing it is because they suggest too much." O'Neill gives direction to their suggestiveness and so makes the denotation possible. He achieves the kind of recreation that we found lacking in the references to Nietzsche in *Lazarus Laughed*.

Because the dialogue is shaped around the poem, Swinburne's words are at once impersonal and dreadfully appropriate: more dreadful because impersonal, set apart from the idiosyncratic prose of the appeals spoken, in turn, by the men. Originally, O'Neill included some commentary on the poem in the dialogue and Edmund's voice alternated with Jamie's. In the final draft, the quotation is not absorbed into the dialogue in this way. The links between the poem and the dialogue are many but they must be made by the audience:

<table>
<tr><td>

She will not know.
She will not hear.
She will not see.

      surely she,
She too, remembering days and
     words that were,
Will turn a little toward us, . . .

Let us go seaward as the great
     winds go,
Full of blown sand and foam.

</td><td>

You know something in her
does it deliberately—to get
beyond our reach, to be rid
of us, to forget we're alive!
It's as if in spite of loving
us, she hated us.

You must not try to touch
me.
You must not try to hold
me.

The fog was where I
wanted to be . . . to be
alone with myself . . . Out
beyond the harbour, where
the road runs along the
beach . . .

</td></tr>
</table>

The intervening dialogue, with its single words and brief sentences, has its own pattern—three times Mary speaks to herself, three times one of the men attempts to penetrate her consciousness and Jamie says the attempt is futile—but, with its rhythm and rhyme and internal verbal echoes, the poem has a more formal pattern which establishes continuity between the stanzas even though they are separated by dialogue, so that Jamie's voice, speaking it, appears to bind the whole sequence and the four individual voices together. Throughout the play we have been made aware of the part verbal deception and self-deception play in the relationships and we have seen human beings deriving comfort from the very structuring of the words spoken. Now, at the end of the play, when we have comprehended the desolation of the Tyrones, O'Neill permits to characters and to audience the comfort that artistic ordering of experience can give: the minimal comfort of an elegy. An elegy fittingly spoken by the character for whom, of all the Tyrones, there is the least comfort possible.

The Mysterious Effectiveness of the Final Scene of the Play

I have suggested that the ending of *Mourning Becomes Electra* was one of the most convincing signs of the imaginative control which O'Neill would achieve in the late plays. It was in many ways a tour de force imposing order on the play. The unfolding action of *Long Day's Journey into Night* has a greater coherence and the dialogue is more absorbingly complex than that of the earlier play. The ending, when it comes, comes as the culmination of the meanings, the undertones and overtones we have absorbed during the play, and it is couched in words and images made potent by their use within the play. In concluding this discussion of the language of the play, it is important to look at the final sequence which, in its quiet and stillness, is so different from that of *The Iceman Cometh*. The sequence has been praised repeatedly: the method of this study should enable us to put into words some, at least, of the reasons for its extraordinary power.

O'Neill altered act 4 in its second draft to keep Mary off-stage until the last few minutes of the play. In doing so, he increased the suspense of the act and the subsequent impact of Mary's appearance. Throughout the act her entrance is anticipated, by the listening attitude of the men, by their comments on her restless pacing above them and by their very presence on the stage, since we recognize that their vigil must continue until she has become still. If we catch it, the reference to Ibsen's *John Gabriel Borkman* is an appropriate one with its memory of that other familial relationship, its tortured, listening women and its intimacy and destructiveness. The underlying pattern of the action demands Mary's presence for its completion. Edmund and Tyrone have moved three times from hostility to understanding, reaching a deeper level of mutual confidence at each stage. Then, the relationship between the two brothers has been presented with comparable intensification as Jamie has moved from bonhomie to threat, to self-revelation. Each of the three men having in turn exposed his secret thought to one of the others, there is a hiatus. Exhausted, they drowse. The balance in which the characters have been held until now makes Mary's entrance inevitable. But it is also startling because of the way in which it takes place. There is a moment of silence and then Edmund jerks up, listening intently. A burst of light at the back of the stage, when all five bulbs of the chandelier flash on, is followed by a burst of sound, when a Chopin waltz is played on the piano. When Mary appears in the doorway, her hair is long and braided girlishly, she wears a sky blue night gown, and carries a wedding dress. O'Neill succeeds in creating a poetry of theatre here where he failed in *Dynamo*, for all the elaborate machinery of that play, because each visual and aural impression arouses in the audience some memory of the dialogue. Things which through repeated naming have become emblems of the private mythology of the family are suddenly present before us in solid form. Jamie's words, which break the silence, have the force of words which should not have been spoken but, having been, cannot be expunged from the mind and Mary's failure to react to them signifies how dissociated from the present she has become. When she speaks she uses the school-girlish register entirely, "I play *so* badly now. I'm *all* out of practice. Sister Theresa will give me a *dreadful* scolding." She is no longer speaking in the present and looking back to the past but, as the verb tenses show, has moved into that past time which has become her present. There follows the highly patterned passage containing the poem after which Mary speaks her final monologue.

Here, as throughout the play, the verbal and visual level are integrated with each other, so that when words leave off the stage image speaks. Once we have absorbed the impact of Mary's final entrance, the stage picture has significance not because, like that, it is startling or spectacular, but because of the way it complements the dialogue. Watching the final moments of the play, we are scarcely aware of how carefully movement and gesture have been organized and how much they contribute to the feeling of the scene. As can be seen from O'Neill's sketch of this sequence [not reproduced here], the men remain still so that our eyes follow Mary as she crosses from the door to the front of the stage. Mary's seemingly aimless movement, in fact takes her past each of the men in turn, taking our attention with her from one to the other of them. In the single other movement, shortly after Mary's entrance, Tyrone approaches Mary who carries her wedding dress that has lain in the old trunk in the attic and that, described with delight by Mary earlier in the play, had become an emblem of her lost girlhood and her reproach to Tyrone. Because we have experienced this, Tyrone's simple gesture of taking the dress from her and holding it protectively is remarkably moving. When Mary comes to rest it is, as the sketch shows, at the front left corner of the stage which leaves the silent characters at the focal point in the centre. This divides the audience's attention during Mary's final speech and so acts as preparation for the last line of the play.

Whilst Mary speaks her monologue, the audience, listening to her words, observe the speaking silence of the listening men and hear, perhaps, the lingering echo of the poem, "There is no help for all these things are so." They recognize that Mary has given herself over to the past, obliterating her men-folk with her colloquialisms, her girlish intensifiers, her manner of discussing the interview as if it had just taken place. Her naïve and trusting words, "I knew She heard my prayer and would always love me and see no harm ever came to me as long as I never lost my faith in her," are almost unbearable for the stage listeners, and for the audience observing the stage listeners and knowing that their perspective is from a different point in time from hers.

The overwhelming effect of the last four lines of the play comes, I think, because, just when it appears that the play has drawn to its conclusion and has reached some kind of resting place, however dismal, the sentence, "*That was* in the winter of senior year," pushes the interview back into the distant past and returns Mary to the present and the family, from which there can be, after all, no escape for any of the four Tyrones. The quiet ending of the play is not a conclusion but another relentless beginning:

> That was in the winter of senior year. Then in the spring something happened to me. Yes, I remember, I fell in love with James Tyrone and was so happy for a time.

Long Day's Journey into Night

Richard B. Sewall

What keeps *Long Day's Journey into Night* from "dwindling to a sorrowful tale" is [a] capacity for suffering—and for learning from it—on the part of the four Tyrones, the name O'Neill gives his own family in this autobiographical play. (They are: James Tyrone, the actor-father; Mary his wife, far gone in dope; Jamie, the older, wastrel son; and Edmund, O'Neill himself at twenty-three, the would-be writer and incipient consumptive.) Each one, during the long day of the play, goes through a kind of agon, not the lonely ordeal of the hero but inseparable from the ordeal of the family, so inextricably—and fatefully—are these four lives woven. No one dominates the scene; there is no Jobian figure to confront whatever it is that has brought this family to the point of dissolution. One is reminded of the wrangling Karamazovs; but there is no Father Zossima to define the evil and send out his Alyosha to do battle. The fog that thickens during the play is, in one sense, a fitting symbol: these are the "fog people" (as Edmund calls them, including himself), individually all but lost in the fog of temperament until, interacting much as had the Karamazovs, in the very torture of their interaction they have glimpses through the fog to new truth.

The play brings up vividly the question of the involvement of the tragic artist in his own fictions, a quality in contrast to the so-called detachment of the satirist or ironist. The closer to modern times, the more such involvement can be documented. O'Neill made his own involvement poignantly clear. To his wife Carlotta on their twelfth wedding anniversary, he wrote:

From *The Vision of Tragedy* (New Edition, Enlarged). © 1980 by Yale University. Yale University Press, 1980.

> Dearest: I give you the original of this play of old sorrow, written in tears and blood. A sadly inappropriate gift, it would seem, for a day celebrating happiness. But you will understand. I mean it as a tribute to your love and tenderness which gave me the faith in love that enabled me to face my dead at last and write this play—write it with deep pity and understanding and forgiveness for *all* the four haunted Tyrones.
>
> These twelve years, Beloved One, have been a Journey into Light—into love. You know my gratitude. And my love!

"To face my dead at last." This confrontation, the "facing," had a long beginning. (O'Neill was sixty-three when he completed the play.) It was as surely a quest for meaning as any of the great ones of our study. The pattern is familiar: out of the welter of experience, out of the suffering, comes the tragic question, "Why?" In his afflictions, Job sought meaning: "Teach me and I will hold my tongue, and cause me to understand wherein I have erred." Lear asked, "Is there any cause in nature that makes these hard hearts?" And Kalganov, weeping over the degradation of Dmitri, asks, "What can mankind be after this?" When O'Neill calls his family the "four haunted Tyrones," he suggests his own sense of the mystery. Writing the play was the result of his forty-year attempt to pierce it—to "understand" it, as he wrote to Carlotta, and "pity" and "forgive." The "tears and blood" suggest the suffering it cost him.

Each of the Tyrones, as if in turn, indicates the take-off point of O'Neill's quest and, had it not been for the play, the end of it—in fatalism, despair, bitterness. Mary sees them all as prisoners of the past: "None of us can help the things life has done to us. . . . He [Jamie] can't help being what the past has made him. Any more than your father can. Or you [Edmund]. Or I." Edmund would simply deny the problem: "Who wants to see life as it is, if they can help it? That's what I wanted—to be alone with myself in another world where truth is untrue and life can hide from itself." Toward the end, Mary asks a question for them all: "What is it I'm looking for? I know it's something I lost," and we see her husband James "trying to shake off his hopeless stupor." "It's no good, Papa," says Jamie, and quotes Swinburne:

> There is no help, for all things are so,
> And all the world is bitter as a tear.

Or, as Job's wife advised, "Curse God, and die."

But no one curses God, and no one commits suicide. The very stamina of these people is awesome as they survive hour after hour (or so it seems) of the often furious exchange of blame and counterblame. The long day is very long, reaching far into the night. Edmund's "fog people" hardly does justice to their emotional capacity—the bursts of temper, the clashes of temperament, the excruciating self-revelations, and (most impressive) the love and loyalty that, for all the bickering, keep them from disintegration, as individuals and as a family. If none of the characters in the play achieves the "deep pity and understanding and forgiveness" of the note to Carlotta, they all have moments of redemptive insight. This is not to say that the family (or any member of it) is redeemed. There is no assurance that the next day might not be a repetition of this long one; but the play shows, clearly and powerfully, how it might have been. The ultimate perception was O'Neill's: "the faith in love that enabled me to face my dead."

The play opens on an August morning in 1912 with the Tyrones in their New London home near the sea. We are confronted at once with the precariousness of the family situation. As Tyrone and Mary emerge from breakfast, their mood seems happy and loving: Tyrone gives Mary a "playful hug" and calls her "a fine armful." But she is clearly on edge, and she jokes a bit caustically about Tyrone's huge appetite and his inept business dealings. They worry about Edmund's illness and Jamie's failure. When the boys come in, the discords mount, and Tyrone's forced good humor is seen for what it is.

Immediately there is a tiff between Tyrone and Jamie, a prelude to the pattern of encounters to come: blame, counterblame, uneasy truce. It starts with Mary's seemingly innocent remark about Tyrone's snoring; then Jamie's "The Moor, I know his trumpet"; then Tyrone's "If it takes my snoring to make you remember Shakespeare instead of the dope sheet on the ponies, I hope I'll keep on with it." Jamie wants out: "What's all the fuss about? Let's forget it." But one word borrows another: "Yes, forget!" says Tyrone. "Forget everything and face nothing. It's a convenient philosophy if you've no ambition in life except to—." Mary steps in and changes the subject. Truce.

Soon the family is laughing over Edmund's story of old Shaughnessy and his pigs and millionaire Harker's ice pond. But the mood doesn't last. Tyrone suspects the boys, with their "damned Socialist anarchist sentiments," of wanting to get him in trouble with Harker. Mary tries to soothe him. Edmund, in "sudden nervous exasperation," leaves the room; and Mary, "with a strange obstinate set to her face," goes to confer with Bridget the cook. Another truce.

Tyrone and Jamie are left alone, and the stage is set for their first major encounter. The theme, as usual, is guilt. Jamie blames Tyrone for

Edmund's illness: he was too stingy to pay for "a real doctor" when Edmund first got sick. Tyrone counters with the terrible accusation that Jamie, out of jealousy, corrupted Edmund to undermine his health. "That's a lie!" Jamie shouts. "I won't stand for that, Papa! . . . Oh, for Christ's sake, Papa! Can't you lay off me!" For a moment the two touch bottom: the charges could hardly have been worse. But then something new happens. It is as if both men have been shocked into their senses by what they have said—and shocked into their better natures. Tyrone's thoughts turn to Mary and the bad luck that Edmund's illness should come at a time when her own state is so precarious. His voice "grows husky and trembles a little": "It's damnable she should have this to upset her, just when she needs peace and freedom from worry. She's been so well in the two months since she came home. It's been heaven to me. This home has been a home again. But I needn't tell you, Jamie." The two suddenly see eye to eye. A stage direction makes it explicit: "His son looks at him, for the first time with an understanding sympathy. It is as if suddenly a deep bond of common feeling existed between them in which their antagonisms could be forgotten." Jamie says ("almost gently"): "I've felt the same way, Papa."

But, being what they are (O'Neill seems to be saying), they cannot sustain this mood for long. Within seconds they are quarreling again. Jamie picks up the theme of his mother's illness and blames it on Tyrone: he was too stingy to hire a proper doctor at the time of Edmund's birth. Tyrone's furious "That's a lie!" seems likely to lead to violence except for Mary (again), whose unexpected entrance brings about another truce.

And now Mary herself has her turn. She brings act 1 to a close in a flurry of accusations and self-pity. She pours out her heart to Edmund. Everything is Tyrone's fault. He was too stingy to give the family a decent home, with an automobile and nice friends. She is lonely. She is worried about Edmund's health. The family doesn't trust her—they keep spying on her. Edmund's "Mama! Stop it!" is unavailing, and he goes, leaving her alone. As the curtain falls, she is "terribly tense . . . seized by a fit of nervous panic," on the point of another fix. When she reappears in act 2 (noon of the same day), "Her eyes are brighter, and there is a peculiar detachment in her voice and manner." While the others find momentary release in temper and (later) alcohol, she finds it in the detachment of morphine. "The only way," she tells Edmund, "is to make yourself not care," and it is here that she slips into the fatalism that relieves everyone of blame and puts it all on "Life."

But neither she nor the others can rest long in such an evasion. This is important to the student of tragedy; for suffering we can call tragic is not to be resolved that easily. There is an echo here of the tragic Dostoyevskian ethic, so clear with the Karamazovs, that there may be salvation in following one's nature, however violent or however extreme in other ways, to the very end—as Dmitri found "precious metal in the dirt." So it is that violence "becomes" these Tyrones. Mary's combative nature soon reasserts itself, and in the ensuing scenes none of the men escapes. Tyrone, she says, never wanted a home; he should have been a bachelor, with his barrooms and his cheap hotels. Jamie's alcoholism is all his fault, and now he lets the invalid Edmund take a drink: "Do you want to kill him?" she snaps. She turns on Jamie, accusing him of killing her second baby by deliberately exposing him to measles—again, out of jealousy.

Then, alone with Edmund, her favorite, she turns on *him* as the source of all her troubles. It was her illness at his birth that led to the quack doctor who prescribed the morphine. And now it's her worry over his health that has driven her to it again. Suddenly she checks herself, as if shocked by what she has said. She cries ("distractedly"), "But that's no excuse! I'm only trying to explain. It's not an excuse!" ("She hugs him to her—pleadingly.") "Promise me, dear, you won't believe I made you an excuse." But all Edmund can say ("bitterly") is, "What else can I believe?"

And now, in her near-panic, comes her moment of insight and gentleness. She confesses her lies and her guilt. "I don't blame you," she says to Edmund:

> How could you believe me—when I can't believe myself? I've become such a liar. I never lied about anything once upon a time. Now I have to lie, especially to myself. I've never understood anything about it [her dependence on morphine], except that one day long ago I could no longer call my soul my own.

Once started, she experiences a tiny epiphany, a vision of a better time to come. It is as if O'Neill, in his quest, were uncovering in his family unsuspected areas of truth (and beauty and goodness). "Lowering her voice to a strange tone of whispered confidence," she pictures for Edmund a time when she might regain her soul, be forgiven, and be believed.

> But some day, dear, I will find it again—some day when you're all well, and I see you healthy and happy and successful, and I don't have to feel guilty any more—some day when the Blessed Virgin Mary forgives me and gives me back the faith in Her love and pity I used to have in my convent days, and I can pray to Her again—when She sees no one in the world can believe in

me even for a moment any more, then She will believe in me, and with Her help it will be so easy. I will hear myself scream with agony, and at the same time I will laugh because I will be so sure of myself.

But this mood doesn't last, either, and like all such moments in the play it is ambivalent. It may have been partly a pose for Edmund's sake. He "remains hopelessly silent," and she concludes curtly, "Of course, you can't believe that, either." Alone a moment later as the scene ends, she is glad the others are gone, glad "to get rid of them." "Then Mother of God," she asks, "why do I feel so lonely?" Pose or no pose, she speaks the plain truth here: she can't get along without her family. Nor can they get along without her.

One simple criterion of tragedy lies in the question, How does our first view of the protagonist (in this case the family) differ from what we see at the end? Has there been a gain, if only minimal, in humanity, self-knowledge, wisdom, insight—all that we have subsumed under the notion of perception? What has been won from "the fine hammered steel of woe"?

When, at the end of act 2, the Tyrones disperse for the afternoon, there seems no good reason, except food and shelter, why they should ever assemble again. Each has said enough, one would think, to make further relations impossible. It is no wonder that when Tyrone and Edmund reappear at dinner time (act 3) they have had a lot to drink. (When Jamie shows up at midnight, in act 4, he is drunk.) Hearing their voices, Mary says, "Why are they coming back? They don't want to." And only a few moments later, when the bickering starts all over again, Tyrone says, "Oh, for the love of God! I'm a fool for coming home!" But here they are, together again. As the two men come in, Mary says to herself that she'd "much rather be alone" but in the next breath ("pathetically relieved and eager") adds, "Oh, I'm so glad they've come! I've been so horribly lonely!" What is it at the very end of the play, when the three men sit in silence during Mary's long soliloquy, that gives the scene, as here in this reunion for dinner, a power that goes beyond pathos? How in the last two acts and especially in the final scene does the family transcend itself, leaving us not so much in tears as in awed silence?

The progress, or "journey," of the play is toward a deeper understanding of each others' nature on the part of the four Tyrones. What they go through—what they put themselves through—is hardly heroic suffering. There are no Jobian afflictions, no state is threatened, no fear (except Edmund's illness) for life or limb. What takes place is all *within*—within the confines of the Tyrone living room, within a single day, within the family (Cathleen, the maid, is the only outsider and has no idea of what is going on). The only intrusions from the outside world are the doctor's verdict on Edmund and the sound of the foghorn and the fog itself, which intensifies the fierce concentration of the scene. "It hides you from the world and the world from you," Mary says. The last two acts reiterate the themes already stated—Tyrone's tightfistedness, Mary's addiction, Jamie's jealousy of Edmund, the strange mixture of emotions each member of the family has for the others: pride and shame, love and hate, contempt and admiration. What is new is the degree of understanding each of them achieves. The climax comes in the alcoholic unburdenings of the men and in Mary's dope-induced finale at the end, but not before the old recriminations have gone back and forth in bitterness and (twice) in physical violence. It is as if the truth has had to wait until every other route (and they themselves) has been exhausted. They have had to find out that the endless blame-laying was a dead-end, that there would be no release until they could look within themselves and be honest to what they saw. This is the true within-ness of the play, the true suffering.

It is here that the magnitude of the play—and of the characters—lies. Nothing would have happened had they not been capable of submitting themselves to each other, of undergoing the agony not only of self-disclosure but of listening to the disclosures of the others. No one walks out and slams the door. They bear it out to the end—and the end is not bitter.

The sequence begins, as we have seen, with Mary's confession to Edmund, who listens in silence. What he learns comes out later as he and his father talk about Mary's condition during their never-finished game of cards at the beginning of act 4. Edmund stumbles on a major insight:

> The hardest thing to take [he tells his father] is the blank wall she builds around her. Or it's more like a bank of fog in which she hides herself. Deliberately, that's the hell of it! You know something in her does it deliberately—to get beyond our reach, to be rid of us, to forget we're alive! It's as if, in spite of loving us, she hated us!

There is a moment of calm as Tyrone "remonstrates gently": "Now, now, lad. It's not her. It's the damned poison." But the damned poison, Edmund points out ("in bitter accusation") is not her fault: "I know damned well she's not to blame! And I know who is! You are! Your damned stinginess! . . . Jesus, when I think of it I hate your guts!" Then comes more vindictive rage until he, too, near bottom, comes to his senses—and to the same insight he had about his mother: that human beings are capable of loving and hating at the same time. "I didn't mean it, Papa. I'm like Mama, I can't help liking you, in spite of everything." Later in act 4, after Jamie's shocking confession that it was indeed true that he had intentionally corrupted Edmund, he too finds himself saying, "But don't get the wrong idea, Kid. I love you more than I hate you."

As the card game goes on, we realize that the bottom has not quite been reached. It is not until Edmund, "bursting with anger," his "voice trembling with rage" and "shaken by a fit of coughing," accuses his father of wanting to save money by sending him to a state institution that Tyrone himself is shocked into his better nature. Now, as "his head bows" and "he stares dully at the cards on the table," he talks "without resentment": "A stinking old miser. Well, maybe you're right." And he launches into a long confession in an attempt to explain himself—his poverty-stricken youth in Ireland, the struggle to establish himself in America, his early years in the theatre and his "good bad luck" in finding "the big moneymaker" (*The Count of Monte Cristo*). The stage directions indicate the mixture of "guilty contrition," "self-contempt," "drunken peevishness," "grim humor," even sentimental nostalgia ("He wipes the tears from his eyes"), and (finally) bitterness: "What the hell was it I wanted to buy, I wonder, that was worth—Well, no matter. It's a late day for regrets." Edmund is "moved, stares at his father with understanding," and says ("slowly"), I'm glad you've told me this, Papa. I know you a lot better now."

One by one, each member of the family goes through the same harrowing process. Now it's Edmund's turn. "You've just told me some high spots in your memories," he says to his father. "Want to hear mine?" What follows is a long, lyric reminiscence of his life at sea. He recalls two episodes when, "for a second," there was "meaning." The first was on a square rigger bound for Buenos Aires, driving along at fourteen knots under a full moon in the Trades. "I became drunk with the beauty and singing rhythm of it," he says, "and for a moment I lost myself—actually lost my life." He became one with the "white sails and flying spray," he *became* "beauty and rhythm . . . moonlight and the ship and the high dim-starred sky." He felt "peace and unity and wild joy." He "belonged . . . to Life itself! To God, if you want to put it that way." The second moment was on a steamship of the American Line, on lookout in the dawn watch—a "moment of ecstatic freedom . . . the peace, the end of the quest, the last harbor, the joy of belonging to a fulfillment beyond men's lousy, pitiful, greedy fears and hopes and dreams!" In such moments it seems as if a veil were drawn back: "For a second you see—and seeing the secret, are the secret." But the veil drops back again and "you are alone, lost in the fog again, and you stumble on toward nowhere, for no good reason!" At this point, "he grins wryly" by way of ironic comment on his ultimate confession:

> It was a great mistake, my being born a man. I would have been much more successful as a seagull or a fish. As it is, I will always be a stranger who never feels at home, who does not really want and is not really wanted, who can never belong, who must always be a little in love with death!

Bitter as his conclusion is, he is blaming no one but himself, and his candor brings him and his father to a moment of understanding. Tyrone "stares at him—impressed." "Yes, there's the makings of a poet in you all right." Then, "protesting uneasily": "But that's morbid craziness about not being wanted and loving death." Edmund, perhaps noting the uneasiness of his father's protest, ignores the morbidness and picks up the matter of the poet:

> The *makings* of a poet. No. . . . I couldn't touch what I tried to tell you just now. I just stammered. That's the best I'll ever do. I mean, if I live. Well, it will be faithful realism, at least. Stammering is the native eloquence of us fog people.

Whether O'Neill actually thought this about himself at age twenty-three, and the way his career belied it, are matters that go beyond the play. What happens in the play is that the moment of harmony between father and son is interrupted by Jamie, who comes in drunk. "Get him to bed, Edmund," says Tyrone. "I'll go out on the porch. He has a tongue like an adder when he's drunk. I'd only lose my temper."

The scene that follows is Jamie's. It's his turn now. No great nature is revealed, but there are surprises, like Dmitri's parting words to Alyosha, "Love Ivan!" He is more than the "drunken hulk" his father calls him. His course during the scene is uneven, but it follows the pattern made familiar by the others. From the moment he enters ("Oh, hello, Kid. I'm as drunk as a fiddler's bitch") he is refreshingly honest. He talks frankly but compassionately about his whore, Fat Violet, and, drunk as he is, he is concerned about Edmund: "I know, Kid, it's been a lousy day for you." And then "in vino veritas" (he uses the phrase), it all comes out: his jealousy of Edmund from the first—"Mama's baby and Papa's pet!"; his deliberate attempt to pull Edmund down with him: "Mama and Papa are right. I've been a rotten bad influence. And worst of it is, I did it on purpose"; his love-hate of Edmund; and finally his own explanation, which lays blame on no one but himself: "Can't help it. I hate myself. Got to take revenge. On everyone else. Especially you."

Jamie doesn't repent or promise to reform. He warns Edmund to be on his guard—he'd still stab him in the back "at the first chance I get." He simply tells the truth: "Remember I warned you—for your sake. Give me credit. Greater love hath no man than this, that he saveth his brother from himself." And finally, before sinking into a drunken doze: "Don't die on me. You're all I've got left. God bless you, K.O."

Tyrone, having overheard the last part of the talk, comes in from the porch. "His face is stern and disgusted but at the same time pitying." Looking down on Jamie "with a bitter sadness," he says, "A sweet spectacle for me! My first-born, who I hoped would bear my name in honor and dignity, who showed such brilliant promise!" Edmund, who has hardly noticed Tyrone's entrance, finally breaks his silence: "Keep quiet, can't you, Papa?"

Pity touched with awe is the mood of the final scene. The family has resisted all the forces that would pull it apart. Mary, who has been moving about upstairs for some time and causing anxious remarks from the men, is heard playing the piano, awkwardly, like a schoolgirl. She suddenly appears "in a sky-blue dressing gown," carrying her wedding dress. She is lost in morphine. Jamie's sardonic comment, "The Mad Scene. Enter Ophelia!" infuriates the other two. Edmund slaps him across the mouth, and Tyrone blurts out, "The dirty blackguard! His own mother . . . I'll kick him out in the gutter tomorrow, so help me God." But Jamie's quick admission—"All right, Kid. Had it coming. But I told you how much I'd hoped—" and his sobbing breaks the anger of his father, who pleads, "Jamie, for the love of God, stop it!" It is Mary's quiet, girl-like, detached presence that quiets the men. The rest of the play, save for Jamie's lugubrious quotations from Swinburne, is Mary's. She has, quite literally, the last word.

She moves about the stage like a sleepwalker, talking to herself, ignoring the others. Tyrone, "in anguish," gently takes the wedding dress from her, which she relinquishes "with the shy politeness of a well-bred young girl toward an elderly gentleman who relieves her of a bundle." The men, for all their drinking, are strangely sober. When Mary speaks, "they freeze into silence again, staring at her." Their first reaction, as she proceeds to act out "the mad scene," is hopelessness, and it is here that Jamie says, "It's no good, Papa," and quotes Swinburne. Tyrone gives up: "Oh, we're fools to pay any attention. It's the damned poison. . . . Pass me that bottle,

Jamie. And stop reciting that damned morbid poetry. I won't have it in my house."

This turns out to be the last skirmish. They all pour drinks. As they are about to drink, there is an important stage direction: "Tyrone lifts his glass and his sons follow suit mechanically, but before they can drink Mary speaks and they slowly lower their drinks to the table, forgetting them." From here on, the men are under her spell. She "stares dreamily before her. Her face looks extraordinarily youthful and innocent." She reminisces about her days in the convent, about her talk with Mother Elizabeth, "so sweet and good," about praying to the Virgin and finding "peace again because I knew she heard my prayer." The men sit motionless and silent.

There is nothing "great" here, but there is a vision, dope-induced as it is, of the good (and true and beautiful). At least we see what might have been—and recall Alyosha's pastoral charge to the boys at the end of *The Brothers Karamazov*, which, if nothing else, made clear the values missing in that family. Neither Alyosha nor Mary brings about radical change. But when Alyosha talked, the boys stopped quarreling; and when Mary begins her soliloquy, the men put down their drinks and listen. Mary's final sentences end the play in a kind of ironic benediction: "That was in the winter of senior year. Then in the spring something happened to me. Yes, I remember. I fell in love with James Tyrone and was so happy for a time." As the curtain falls, only Tyrone "stirs in his chair."

Such was the situation in the O'Neill family, the play says, in "August, 1912." What "haunted" them? Nothing, surely, like the Curse on the House of Atreus, or a regicide, or the ancestral sins that so haunted Hawthorne. No one killed an albatross or was dismembered by a whale. Perhaps O'Neill's word "haunted" is to be explained mainly by the facts of inherited temperament—the family Irishness, of which he makes a good deal: the bursts of temper, the moodiness, the sudden extremes of emotion, the flamboyance and love of talk, the touch of the visionary in each of them, even Jamie. But temperament isn't all; it doesn't determine everything. O'Neill makes it clear that the fault (Tyrone quotes the passage) is not in their stars. And like all tragic faults (or flaws) it involves the exercise of the will.

Tragedy, to O'Neill, ennobled in art what he called man's "hopeless hopes." If life in 1912 seemed hopeless, something in him—the dream, the vision, the hope, the very Irish vitality that is awesome in the play—kept him going, with the results we all know. There is something here of the hopeless hope that kept young Quentin Compson burrowing into the story of his family in an attempt to understand and perhaps forgive; but we know that in *The Sound and the Fury* Faulkner has his young hero, unable to bear the burden, commit suicide. O'Neill bore it out to the end. He was once reported as saying, "I couldn't ever be negative about life. On that score you've got to decide YES or NO. And I'll always say YES." There was a good deal of the Greek in him, as well as the Irish. "To O'Neill tragedy had the meaning the Greeks gave it, and it was their classic example that he tried to follow. He believed with the Greeks that tragedy always brought exaltation, 'an urge [he once said] toward life and ever more life.'" Tragedy, he said, brought men "to spiritual understandings and released them from the petty greeds of everyday existence." Whatever it was that haunted his family—and him—he found release in his lifelong dedication to the tragic drama, to the dream, he said, that kept man "fighting, willing —living."

Eugene O'Neill: The Life Remembered

John Orr

O'Neill's work . . . goes beyond questions of political idealism and disenchantment. It expresses a profound concern with the impact of capitalism on the American way of life, an impact which has persisted throughout the century despite, and sometimes because of, the vagaries of political opposition. While revolutionary idealism has been volatile and at times perfidious, the system to which it is a response has prevailed permanently in all areas of life. In O'Neill's mature work this was the guarantor of tragic alienation and its transformation to a full realised tragic strife. But the work was historical within the span of O'Neill's lifetime since the constancy of his opposition to the American way of life was tempered by the sense of lost promise. The latter gives the vital historical dimension to the former which is both historical and contemporary, a part of time past and time present and also of our own age, time future, when the themes of the play strike a chord of instant recognition through their profoundly prophetic qualities.

This holds equally of *Long Day's Journey into Night* which is usually seen as a profoundly personal statement about personal matters because of its immense autobiographical content. The concentration on the nuclear family and the use of the family living-room as the single setting could easily be seen as a relapse into traditional naturalism after the bold experimentation of the earlier plays. But this reversion to the classical Unities, accomplished by O'Neill with a remarkable rigour, expresses with an even greater intensity than *Iceman* the alienation from bourgeois life so necessary

From *Tragic Drama and Modern Society: Studies in the Social and Literary Theory of Drama from 1870 to the Present.* © 1981 by John Orr. Macmillan, 1981.

to modern tragedy. Such an alienation could not be created if the audience merely witnessed the personalised disintegration of the bourgeois family. There has to be something more. What this is, remains at first sight difficult to pin down. It is not enough to say the Tyrones are not a typical bourgeois family. There is a more profound sense of displacement at the centre of middle-class life and family life in general which is built up as the drama progresses to the point of tragic climax, where O'Neill shows that there is no real centre to family life at all.

The opening scene starts on a deceptive note of casual domestic happiness. James Tyrone affectionately teases his wife, Mary, about her putting on weight. From the dining room the voices of their two sons Jamie and Edmund can be heard in laughter. But soon the image of domestic contentment has all but evaporated. In its place there is quarrel and recrimination, wounding and suffering, accusation and confession. These are as much the consequence of tragic alienation as its cause, and in themselves do not lead to irreparable breakdown. No one deserts the household, no one is murdered within its walls. The conflict is cyclical and recurrent, an echo of old wounds and grievances and a renewal of them. In modern theatre, this recycled animosity usually derives from the sense of imprisonment it engenders in the household's three-walled room. But in O'Neill the household is not a bourgeois prison and recriminations do not achieve pathos by being bounced off the walls. The Tyrone's house is a rented summer house which they will soon leave, and while the action never leaves it, that action bespeaks a deep rootlessness. The trapped family does not belong there, and never has.

The life of the family has always been based on the theatre, constantly travelling from one town to another, and from one hotel to another, its head an ageing matinée idol whose hour of glory is past. The two sons have inherited the same restlessness. The location provides only a provisional unity, a temporary homecoming, and the domestic setting has no domestic spirit. The mother, who as a typical middle-class woman is expected to provide the aura of domesticity and homeliness, pays ritual homage to her expected role and condemns her family for failing to support her. They have, it is true, all the material possessions—servants, car and chauffeur, and even investments in property. But Mary Tyrone pinpoints the anguished lack in a tirade against her husband:

> Oh, I'm so sick and tired of pretending that this is a home! You won't help me! You won't put yourself out the least bit! You really don't know how to act in a home! You don't really want

one! You never have wanted one!—never since the day we were married! You should have remained a bachelor and lived in second-rate hotels and entertained your friends in barrooms! (*She adds rather strangely as if she were talking aloud to herself rather than to Tyrone.*) Then nothing would ever have happened.

Yet her accusation concluded in the last line is followed by an even more disturbing statement. It then becomes clear, despite her periodic protestations, her concern over Edmund's health and her bitter attacks on her husband, that she has abdicated from her conventional family role and long ceased trying to create a "home."

In the dramatic development of the play a remarkable switch takes place. Ostensibly the main plot concerns the fate of Edmund and the consequences of his tubercular illness. But as concern with his illness intensifies within the family, so gradually the focus switches to his mother and the deeper illness which has already destroyed her. As her entreaties of "maternal solicitude" toward her son increase, it becomes increasingly clear that her anxiety for his welfare is an attempt to ignore the seriousness of the illness. She wishes no external source of anxiety to impinge upon her. The more she protests her maternal and conjugal caring, the more she tries to wrap herself in a cocoon of her own making, and to seek out protective oblivion. Through her opium addiction she has fled household and family into the interior of her imagination, and she can no longer be called upon as the necessary anchor for family life. The void is terrifying because it underlies the recognisable male vices—the drinking of father and sons alike, the whoring of Jamie, the meanness of James Tyrone, and the introverted agonies of Edmund. All show a greater rootedness in the world than the tragic withdrawals of Mary.

Edmund's bohemian decadence, his fragile sensibility, and his contempt for bourgeois normality give him all the credentials of a tragic hero, a candidate for death through fatal illness in a family which can neither truly care nor understand. In this respect, Mary's rebuke to him is like that of an outraged mother to an overgrown child. But when Edmund jokes about the possibility of his death, the outrage turns into panic, revealing in her the malaise she attributes to her son:

> MARY (*suddenly turns to them in a confused panic of frightened anger*). I won't have it! (*She stamps her foot.*) Do you hear, Edmund! Such morbid nonsense! Saying you're going to die! It's the books you read! Nothing but sadness and death! Your father

shouldn't allow you to have them! And some of the poems you've written yourself are even worse! You'd think you didn't want to live! A boy of your age with everything before him! It's just a pose you get out of books! You're not really sick at all.

The next minute she will be teasing Edmund affectionately telling him he wants "to be petted and spoiled and made a fuss over." But the focus has switched in that moment from the iconoclastic poet to the mother who acts out the role of motherhood while rejecting it in its totality, devoutly wishing that it had never happened to her.

The family loyalty which underlies the family conflicts is in some senses remarkable. Jamie and Edmund are both grown men, both old enough to have broken all family ties if such ties should interfere with their personal ambitions. The loyalty cannot just be explained by compassion, which is so often betrayed, nor by conventional forms of dependence. The family stays together because of the connecting links between the different forms of alienation which each of them suffer, forms which also link the two generations, some present at the family's inception and others developing through its prodigal sons. The dramatic development of the play must therefore move in the direction of the past, of what underlies the present predicament. Here the figure of James Tyrone is significantly different from the Strindbergian patriarch O'Neill created in a number of his earlier plays. He is certainly head of the household, and certainly the most socially conventional member of the family, his investments in property clearly intended as a means of attaining greater wealth and respectability. But his family background and acting career separate him from bourgeois convention in ways which have a lasting and irreversible impact upon the Tyrone family.

The mode of dramatic revelation works toward establishing a truer identity for the respectable head of the household. Tyrone is a combination of his Irish background and its peasant origins and his successful acting career. According to O'Neill's stage directions he should be "a simple unpretentious man whose inclinations are still close to his humble beginnings and his Irish farmer forebears." Yet at the same time "the actor shows in all his unconscious habits of speech, movement and gesture. These have the quality of belonging to a studied technique." The physicality of the man embodies directly the two main aspects of his life, and both belie his middle-class persona even when both at times are used to express the most conventional and moralistic of attitudes. Of key importance here is Mary's account of her first meeting with Tyrone, as a great matinée idol playing

Shakespeare and French melodrama. The description comes in the form of a reverie, recounted to Cathleen the servant girl when the opium begins to take effect:

> My father took me to see him at first. It was a play about the French Revolution and the leading part was a nobleman. I couldn't take my eyes off him. I wept when he was thrown into prison—and then was so mad at myself because I was afraid my eyes and nose would be red. My father had said we would go backstage to his dressing room after the play and we did . . . And he was handsomer than my wildest dream, in his make-up and his nobleman's costume that was so becoming to him. He was different from all ordinary men, like someone from another world.

This of course portrays the romantic infatuation of a young girl. But it is more. It is an image held and fixed in Mary's mind for the rest of her life, and intensified by the resort to opium. In her withdrawn world where as she claims "only the past when you were happy is real," the image has more power over her than any of the difficulties of her present life. She must make it immune from the meanness of her husband, the drunkenness and whoring of Jamie, and the illness of Edmund. The source of the image is itself of vital social importance. The performance which so captivates her is that of a doomed aristocratic hero. The aura of nobility absent from the drama of American life in O'Neill's own plays, is captured reflexively through the grand roles from which James Tyrone derived his acting reputation. Only the theatre in America, by importing plays from Europe, can recreate the aura of nobility which the New World cannot propagate of its own accord. But the theatrical aura of the noble which captures Mary's heart is far removed from the reality of the actor's life, the sordid existence of "week after week of one-night stands, in dirty rooms of filthy hotels, eating bad food." Far from domesticating that aura, marriage and family life take second place to the debilitating means of producing it. There is no stable family life and no fixed abode. The romanticism of living with a famous actor is dissipated with Edmund's difficult birth and the subsequent addiction to opium, recommended to Mary by a quack doctor to alleviate her pain. As Tyrone aspires from his rigid Catholic standpoint to the wealth and material success promised by the American Dream, Mary Tyrone becomes the victim of the arduous and unconventional means through which alone he has any chance of attaining it.

The theatrical image of the doomed nobleman cannot be reduced to a cosmetic product of Tyrone's acting ability. The melodrama at which Tyrone was so powerfully adept, and which O'Neill in real life hated so much, drew its strength from another social source which went far beyond theatrical skill. That strength came from the desperation of poverty in a first-generation Irishman who knew the exploitation of his class and race at first hand. That he has to remind Edmund of it, shows how far it can be overlooked within the space of a single generation. But its significance is still with all of them:

> There was no damned romance in our poverty. Twice we were evicted from the miserable hovel we call home, with my mother's few sticks of furniture thrown out into the street, and my mother and sisters crying. I cried, too, though I tried hard not to. At ten years old. There was no more school for me. I worked twelve hours a day in a machine shop learning to make files. A dirty barn of a place where rain dripped through the roof, where you roasted in summer, and there was no stove in winter and your hands got numb with cold, where the only light came through two small filthy windows, so on grey days I'd have to sit bent over with my eyes almost touching the files in order to see! . . . It was in those days I learned to be a miser. A dollar was worth so much then. And once you've learned a lesson it's hard to unlearn. You have to look for bargains and if I took this state farm for a bargain you have to forgive me.

His speech is a defence of the attempt to find Edmund a cheap sanatorium and so gravely risk his son's health. But the emphasis on poverty also strikes an appropriate balance with Mary's drugged reminiscence, showing the material basis upon which the future matinée idol had managed to survive before his acting career. The dialectic of the noble and the proletarian is thus revealed in the contrast between the acting persona which captivates his female admirers and the grinding poverty of an exploited child immigrant desperately trying to support his fatherless family. It is only when this dual background is in focus that Tyrone's grotesque maladaptation to the role of man of property makes any sense. Tyrone's thrift is not that of the Protestant Ethic, and in a strictly capitalistic sense he has never come to realise the value of money at all. At different stages in the life of the family, its two tragic figures, Edmund and Mary have suffered immeasurably from his meanness and miscalculation, not because he is a ruthless capitalist but because he is hardly a capitalist at all.

The intense emphasis on individual and family predicament enabled O'Neill to transcend the Shavian drama of social reform and to make personal affliction universally tragic. Such affliction, though it can be labelled in conventional sociological terms as alcoholism, anomie, drug addiction, etc., is ultimately immune to the ethos of Welfare Statism even though superficially the drama can be misread as a series of connected social problems. For the personal predicament of each family member is too powerful for existing society to alter. Rational enlightenment, concocted as a formula for moral reform of self, has no place. Instead O'Neill creates the most intense figural dimension of loss to be found in modern tragedy. It is conveyed in the memorable words of Mary, lost in drugged reminiscence:

> None of us can help the things life has done to us. They're done before you realise it, and once they're done they make you do other things until at last everything comes between you and what you'd like to be, and you've lost your true self for ever.

In fact, the dramatic and figural development of the play are inseparable. They both move simultaneously toward a sense of ultimate closure, the closure of darkness and night. The natural coming of darkness is complemented by the withdrawal of Mary Tyrone into the recesses of dream where she dwells on the life she has lost for ever and condemns without exception the life she is obliged to live.

The dual movement is of course also a movement from alienation to climactic strife, and here a crucial mediating element in the composition of the drama's tragic space interposes itself. This is the enshrouding fog which in act 3, at half-past six in the evening, has rolled in from the Sound like "a white curtain drawn down outside the windows." The apparent freedom of setting and space is suddenly removed. The vista onto the ocean is blotted out, and the freedom of the New World which O'Neill had embraced so subversively with polar images of openness and closure, is finally negated. The process of negation is continuous with the earlier work but the openness of dramatic space is finally relinquished. The effect of closure is greater than in *The Iceman* because in the latter the closure is static, whereas in *Long Day's Journey* the effect is progressive. By the beginning of the fourth act, at midnight, the fog appears "denser than ever." There is no outside source of light, the only sound to be heard that of the foghorn operating in the harbour. The setting and substance of the last act are phantasmagorical. The figural sensibility is integrated with the closure of dramatic space. Edmund, who has walked back drunkenly to the house through the fog, links the imprisoning effect of nature to his spiritual yearning for insubstantiality:

> Everything looked and sounded unreal. Nothing was what it is. That's what I wanted—to be alone with myself in another world where truth is untrue and life can hide from itself. Out beyond the harbour where the road runs along the beach, I even lost the feeling of being on land. The fog and the sea seemed part of each other. It was like walking on the bottom of the sea. As if I had drowned long ago. As if I was a ghost beckoning to the fog, and the fog was the ghost of the sea.

This feeling of a trapped alienation containing within it a metaphor of the dispersion of self into nothingness, is a prelude to the entry of a real ghost whose insubstantiality is more real. It is fitting that Edmund should use the metaphor because he both understands it and is at the same time its main victim. The real ghost is his mother who in her world of dreams has rejected him. As he and his father listen to her moving upstairs, he puts it explicitly: "She'll be nothing but a ghost haunting the past by this time. (*He pauses—then miserably.*) Back before I was born." The past she haunts is an alternative fate which excludes all of her family, a haunting dream of girlish innocence and chastity in which she can recall her ambition to become a nun in the days before meeting James Tyrone. The alternative *figura* is realised theatrically with Mary's momentous entry into the room, one of the most powerful moments in all of O'Neill's work. With her wedding gown over her arm and trailing on the floor, her girlish innocence appears as "a marble mask." The entrance is the climax to tragic strife. But the strife is not violent and does not result in death. Her entrance shows her alienation not only from life in general but from her family, and rises above the dissonant chorus of internecine strife in which her menfolk are drunkenly indulging. Jamie sardonically recalls the mad scene with Ophelia. But the reference cannot detract from the emotional intensity of the scene. There is a tragic horror about her remoteness which they and the audience finally recognise. For the father and the two sons, it is a remoteness which annihilates all of them. Mary Tyrone has rolled back the years to a chaste girlhood devoid of the cares of courtship, marriage and childbirth, and only by excluding them from her dream world can she continue to cherish any fragment of human hope.

The contrast with Hedda Gabler and Nora Clitheroe is strong and apt. Whereas Hedda attempts to manipulate the men around her, Mary tries to repudiate their very existence. While Nora's madness arises from the feeling that her husband has deserted her, Mary Tyrone's madness and addiction arises from the fact of never being able to escape husband and family. Opium replaces the loved one she cannot find in her own family, though under the spell of it she is no longer able to give it a name: "Something I need terribly. I remember when I had it I was never lonely or afraid. I can't have lost it for ever. I would die if I thought that. Because then there would be no hope." The hope continues in the dream of a life she could have led which only opium can sustain and which induces an absolute withdrawal into self. Watching her, her family feel not only pity but at the same time the horror of being liquidated themselves by the process which removes her from them.

With the completion of this play, O'Neill's major work, there is a movement full circle in modern tragedy to the radical closure of the tragic space within. The darkness is deeper than any other twentieth-century play, and has the intensity of Lear. The glimpse of hope which is necessarily allowed to remain, becomes no more than a transient moment of the life remembered. The lost promise is retained in the haunting memory, but the price of reestablishing it as an imaginary universe is insanity. For the sane, no matter how disaffected, how alienated, it can only be a very brief moment of revelation. Confronted by the madness of his mother, Edmund's Nietzschean vision of a fusion of soul and cosmos is eloquent and far reaching, but when all is told, merely a fragment. He recalls the experience of sailing on a square rigger bound for Buenos Aires:

> I lay on the bowsprit, facing astern, with the water foaming into spume under me, the masts with every sail white in the moonlight towering above me. I became drunk with the beauty and singing rhythm of it, and for a moment I lost myself—actually lost my life. I was set free! I dissolved in the sea, became white sails and flying spray, became beauty and rhythm, became moonlight and the ship and the dim-starred sky! I belonged without past or future, within peace and unity and a wild joy, within something greater than my own life, or the life of Man, to life itself!

But each of these moments is transitory:

> For a second you see —and seeing the secret, you are the secret. For a second there is meaning! And then the hand lets the veil fall and you are alone, lost in the fog again, and you stumble on towards nowhere for no good reason.

The brief moment of hope becomes wider and more universal but the darkness which soon envelops it is also more powerful. Without mentioning it explicitly anywhere, O'Neill among all modern writers has produced the most prophetic vision of human extinction on a scale made possible by nuclear war. The personal darkness is also the darkness of the universe as a whole. It is a darkness more intense and resounding than anything Beckett subsequently created during a period when the possibility became widely known, and it ranges back and forth without constraint from the personal to the social and from the social to the universal. The night of O'Neill's play is the darkness of the twentieth century fully brought to light. Concentrated in the life of one family, it explodes outwards to embrace the whole of modern civilisation.

The Retreat behind Language

C. W. E. Bigsby

O'Neill maintains an ambiguous response to the mode in which he writes. His characters are forever quoting—usually from poets, on occasion from playwrights. In doing so they are attempting an ironic distancing from themselves. Apt or not, the words they speak are not their own. They are retreating behind language, a language which has already been shaped by other consciousnesses. Art itself thus becomes a kind of mask, another protective device. And this was the paradox of his art. The touch of the poet, which is the mark of so many of his characters, betrays a desire to reshape the world which is equally the origin of that evasion of the real which is at times the essence of their self-betrayal. The writer, as in *The Arabian Nights*, is in effect staving off death. The story becomes life giving or at least death defeating. O'Neill's characters are poets manqués. Language is the essence of their resistance.

Greek and Shakespearean tragedy assumed the existence of a moral universe in which justice would eventually exert its supremacy. It took for granted that man was a part of an homogeneous world and that to place oneself in opposition to that world was to invite destruction. O'Neill's characters inhabit a very different world. For him there was a fundamental gulf between the individual and the world, a gulf which he and his characters sought to close through holistic schemata, through religion, politics or a Nietzschean assertion of pagan continuities.

From *A Critical Introduction to Twentieth-Century American Drama, 1900–1940*, vol. 1. © 1982 by Cambridge University Press.

In the synopsis which he wrote at Le Plessis and which is dated June 1939, O'Neill tried out various titles for his new play. Two of these were *The Long Day's Retirement* and *The Long Day's Retreat*. Both titles identify a basic theme of the play and, indeed, of O'Neill's work. For the play is patterned around the various strategies of retreat adopted by the tortured Tyrone family, while, again like so much of his work, the rhetorical method of the play is patterned on statements made and then retracted, sentences which are withdrawn before they are completed, cruelties interdicted by compassion, kindnesses unmade by bitterness. Theirs is a world of incompleted gestures, needs never satisfied, longings never realised.

The whole Tyrone family is in retreat. They live in a house set back from the harbour road on the fringe of the town (O'Neill's sketch for the house is an almost exact reproduction of his family's New London home). They seem to have no real friends. Their isolation is underlined by the fog that swirls in from the sea, separating them more completely and acting as an image of that progressive withdrawal from the world which is in some ways the subject of the play and which is embodied most directly in the figure of Mary Tyrone, originally to have been called Stella. Her gradual eclipse lies at the centre of *Long Day's Journey into Night*.

Her retreat had begun long before. On the death of her first child, a death for which she blamed herself and her husband since she had left the baby to join him on tour, she had conceived James Jr as a way of blotting out the fact of that death and denying that guilt. Thus, ironically, James's birth had been the first stage in a progressive retirement from self-knowledge, from personal responsibility and from the meaning of death. And when a quack doctor gives her morphine to relieve the pain of that birth he opens another avenue of escape.

When the play begins, having successfully withdrawn from her addiction for several months, she has just returned to her dependency, frightened by Edmund's illness. But the drug only provides the most tangible evidence of her retreat. Her most obvious resource is a retreat into language. Her family's bitterness and suspicion make them unavailable for consolation, so that she staves off self-awareness with a nervous loquacity as her hands flutter with an equally aimless movement. "I know it's useless to talk," she admits, "but sometimes I feel so lonely." Her solipsism, however, is merely an intense form of an isolation which is more generally applicable. As O'Neill indicates in his scenario for the play, she and her husband "stare helplessly at each other, the helpless stare of a man and woman who have known each other and never known each other." O'Neill's, like Tennessee

Williams's characters, are sentenced to solitary confinement inside their own skins for life.

The intensification of isolation is given concrete form in Mary's retreat into the spare room, always a sign of the detachment, and will for detachment, which comes from her resort to morphine. And this movement is intensified by the fog which stands as an image of her withdrawal. Indeed in his notes O'Neill outlines what he called the "weather progression" of the play. The action begins on a fine morning. The fog is clearing. In the second act, as his notes indicate, the sunshine dims and with it Tyrone's optimism. In the third act the first distant sound of a fog horn acts as an ominous sign which Tyrone still resists, hoping that the fog will stay out at sea. But in the fourth act it finally arrives and encloses them. For Mary and for Edmund it is welcome, for the former because it makes concealment possible, for the latter because it destroys the distinction between the real and the illusory.

But if her retreat is described in terms of present reality, a kind of horizontal schema, it also has a vertical dimension. Unable to face a future consisting of her own addiction and guilt and her son's illness, she retreats into the past. The dead son becomes the only son she had loved because he represents the unambiguous. Beyond that she recalls the days of her courtship and trails her wedding-dress behind her, finding a lyricism in her description of its simple beauty which has disappeared from her own life. And behind that she turns to a religious faith which is the last possible retreat, to the Virgin Mary who conceived without sin and who thus was free of a guilt which in some ways is inseparable from sexual knowledge. What she yearns for, in other words, is innocence, as do all the Tyrones. And in order to assert that innocence they are ready to accuse one another.

The shifting alliances which they form were very much a part of the original plan for the play. Relationships resolve themselves into "battles" (O'Neill's word in the notes for what he called his "New London Play"), and O'Neill reminded himself, in his notes, to ensure that the movement of the play would correspond to these shifting alliances. But this hostility does continuous battle with an ambiguous love, ambiguous because it is both the source of consolation and of pain and as such is an expression of a basic paradox of existence. Hence it is James Tyrone's love for his wife which leads him to want her with him on tour. Yet it is that presence which leads to the death of her child. It is a paradox which baffles and bewilders her and which O'Neill planned that she should only perceive clearly in the final act. His notes for what was to have been a fifth act (he eventually divided the second act into two scenes) read: "Just before end, she *snaps* [*partly illegible*] into awareness again—the trouble is all love each other—so easy to leave if indifferent, or could just hate—but no, we have to love each other—even you, Jamie—when you say wish father would die—oh, I know you mean that at times—I have meant it, too—but you know very well you love and respect, too." It is a realisation which she is not permitted in the final version, a journey towards self-perception and clarity of thought which would have been inconsistent with her clouded mind, her retreat into the past and the pervasive imagery of fog. But it is a perception which still lies at the heart of the play. As it is, the irony is caught more delicately in the final reverie about her youth and her observation that "in the spring something happened to me. Yes, I remember. I fell in love with James Tyrone and was so happy for a time." The ironic implications of a blighted spring, of life turned against itself, were familiar enough. There seems a clear echo of the concluding sentence of *The Sun Also Rises*. But the final image of the play is reminiscent of the stasis of a Beckett play and, indeed, the final moments of *The Iceman Cometh*. For after the emotional turmoil and the unnerving articulateness of the play we are left with silence and immobility. Mary "stares before her in a sad dream. Tyrone stirs in his chair; Edmund and Jamie remain motionless." And there is a sense in which they are involved in an endlessly repeated ritual. Though the play is specifically located in 1912, the characters are in a sense merely re-enacting an archetypal experience. Edmund's attempted suicide had its parallel in the suicide of Tyrone's father while Edmund's tuberculosis reflects that of Mary's mother.

His notion of character remains much as it had been in the earlier plays. It is reactive. It bears the imprint of heredity and environment, though his concern is less naturalistic than metaphysical. And clearly in the context of this family, in which the baby Eugene had died, Edmund has been arbitrarily struck down by illness, and his mother saddled with an addiction which controlled her before she was aware of it, there is a validity granted to Mary's lament that "None of us can help the things life has done to us. They're done before you realize it, and once they're done they make you do other things until at last everything comes between you and what you'd like to be, and you've lost your true self forever." Except, of course, that the true self has no existence outside the ironies generated by the collision between platonic form and reality. Jamie's cynicism, parodied by Edmund—"Everything's in the bag! It's all a frame-up! We're all fall guys and suckers and we can't beat the game"—is inadequate because it presumes no resistant impulse, because it fails to take account of the imperfect but constantly asserted compassion which is in part generated by that sense of shared victimisation. The Catholic faith is seen as purely a retreat from truth, but love, though implicated in the deterministic drive, is not simply anodyne. It operates even in the face of a full knowledge of the real. Nor does it ever become a simple piety, as it does, for example, in the work of James Baldwin, or Tennessee Williams at their weakest. It may be invoked, as it is by Mary, as an excuse for not facing the truth about herself but she is right in refusing to grant her addiction as constituting an adequate definition of her life. As she says to her husband, "We've loved each other! We always will! Let's remember only that, and not try to understand what we cannot understand, or help things that cannot be helped—the things life has done to us we cannot excuse or explain." And it is true that, though love and happiness have not proved synonymous, love does still operate.

And though Mary is the principal focus for the theme of blunted aspirations (the girl who wanted to be a concert pianist and now has crippled hands; who wanted to be a nun and married an actor), the other characters stand as variations on that theme. Tyrone is sensible of having thrown away his chance to be a great actor by settling for material rewards; James is jealous of his brother's talents and has become a pathetic drunk; Edmund's poetic sensibility has been deflected into a self-pitying admiration for other writers, literature itself becoming a retreat. And so the Tyrones cling together, afraid of the future and unable to face the past because that is to remind themselves of a promise which was in part blighted by their own wilfulness as well as by the operation of something they wish to dignify with the name of fate. For the truth is that they all allow absolute authority to the past. As Mary says, "The past is the present, isn't it. It's the future, too. We all try to lie out of that but life won't let us." They, like her, accept the present as itself only as illusion. O'Neill's description of Mary's state could apply equally well to the rest of the family. For they, like her, have "found refuge and release in a dream where present reality is but an appearance to be accepted and dismissed unfeelingly—even with a hard cynicism—or entirely ignored." The only refuge is the past, the world of childhood innocence. Indeed Mary even suggests that it would have been better had Edmund died, for then he would have been spared suffering. Thus life is suffering which can only be avoided by death.

And Edmund himself is attracted by this oblivion—seeing the fog as blotting out the real, removing him from the social context which is the source of his pain. "I didn't meet a soul. Everything looked and sounded unreal. Nothing was what it is. That's what I wanted—to be alone with myself in another world where truth is untrue and life can hide from itself." In other words only by destroying the other can he destroy pain, but by destroying the other he denies himself not only consolation but identity itself. And the logical extension of this is death, literal or figurative. "I even lost the feeling of being on land. The fog and the sea seemed part of each other. It was like walking on the bottom of the sea. As if I had drowned long ago." Alcohol and morphine are simply ways to approximate this death, attempts to annihilate time which is the source of all ironies, for it is that which turns spring into autumn, childhood into adulthood, hope into the frustrated dream.

Man's fate, as O'Neill sees it, is to glimpse order and unity and live with disorder and chaos. As Edmund remarks, "For a second there is meaning! Then the hand lets the veil fall and you are alone, lost in the fog again, and you stumble on towards nowhere for no good reason." This is the absurdist vision against which the individual can only pitch compassion and a poetic sense, a creative reshaping of the world which creates a pro-visional beauty. They all possess a touch of the poet. For them, as for O'Neill, this is the source of meaning, and Edmund's comment on his own talent is essentially O'Neill's description of his own position as a playwright. "The *makings* of a poet. No, I'm afraid I'm like the guy who is always panhandling for a smoke. He hasn't even got the makings. He's got only the habit. I couldn't touch what I tried to tell you just now. I just stammered. That's the best I'll ever do. I mean, if I live. Well, it will be a faithful realism at least. Stammering is the native eloquence for us fog people." The gap between language and experience is akin to the gap between aspiration and fulfilment.

This stands, paradoxically, as O'Neill's most eloquent statement of his own achievement. Having looked for an adequate response to existence he found it in the end in the love with which he was able to approach his wife and his family and in the art with which he faithfully rendered the imper-fections and ironies of the life which had given him such pain (a pain now literally undermining his ability to write), but which had also given him a glimpse of meaning, a sense, finally, of belonging to the world from which he had felt so alienated. For through his art he achieved a loss of self which was transcendence rather than death, a denial of time which was not eva-sion but recognition of higher values.

> I became drunk with the beauty and singing rhythm of it, and
> for a moment I lost myself—actually lost my life. I was set free!
> I dissolved in the sea, became white sails and flying spray, be-
> came beauty and rhythm, became moonlight and the ship and

the dim-starred sky! I belonged, without past or future, within peace and unity and a wild joy, within something greater than my own life, or the life of Man, to Life itself. [And this is] the end of the quest, the last harbour, the joy of belonging to a fulfilment beyond men's lousy, pitiful, greedy fears and hopes and dreams.

And yet they do move closer to truth, admitting to their own failings, to the jealousies, the unrealised dreams which had made them turn against others in preference to facing the guilt which can be located nowhere but in their own hearts.

Chronology

1888   October 16, in New York City, Eugene Gladstone O'Neill, born to James O'Neill, a well-known actor and Ella Quinlan.

1902   O'Neill enters Betts Academy in Stamford, Connecticut.

1906–7   Attends Princeton.

1909   Marries Kathleen Jenkins; goes prospecting for gold in Honduras.

1910   Son Eugene Gladstone O'Neill, Jr., is born. O'Neill sails for Buenos Aires.

1912   Divorces Kathleen Jenkins. Begins work as a reporter for *New London Telegraph*. Publishes poetry. Enters Gaylord Farm, tuberculosis sanatorium, for a six-month stay.

1913   *A Wife for Life* and *The Web*, O'Neill's first plays, are copyrighted.

1914   O'Neill's father helps to pay for the publication of *Thirst*, a volume of five one-act plays.

1916   Provincetown Players produce *Bound East for Cardiff*, *Thirst*, and *Before Breakfast*.

1917   *Fog*, *The Sniper*, *In the Zone*, *The Long Voyage Home*, and *Ile* are produced.

1918   O'Neill marries Agnes Boulton and moves to Cape Cod. *The Rope*, *Where the Cross Is Made*, and *The Moon of the Caribbees* are produced.

1919   *The Dreamy Kid* is produced. Son Shane is born.

1920   *Beyond the Horizon* is produced, and wins the Pulitzer Prize. *Chris Christoferson* (first version of *Anna Christie*), *Exorcism*, *The Emperor Jones*, and *Diff'rent* produced.

1921   *Gold*, *The Straw*, and *Anna Christie* produced. *Anna Christie* wins Pulitzer Prize, O'Neill's second.

1922   *The First Man* and *The Hairy Ape* produced.

1924   *Welded, The Ancient Mariner, All God's Chillun Got Wings, S.S. Glencairn,* and *Desire under the Elms* are produced.

1925   *The Fountain* produced. Daughter Oona is born.

1926   *The Great God Brown* produced. O'Neill receives an honorary Litt.D. from Yale University.

1928   *Marco Millions, Strange Interlude,* and *Lazarus Laughed* are produced. Wins third Pulitzer for *Strange Interlude.* Divorces again.

1929   O'Neill marries Carlotta Monterey. *Dynamo* is produced. Moves to Le Plessis, France.

1931   *Mourning Becomes Electra* is produced.

1932   Returns to U.S. and builds "Casa Genotta," in Sea Island, Georgia.

1933   *Ah, Wilderness!* is produced.

1934   *Days without End* produced.

1936   O'Neill wins the Nobel Prize for Literature.

1937   Moves to California, where he builds "Tao House."

1946   *The Iceman Cometh* is produced.

1947   O'Neill contracts Parkinson's Disease. *A Moon for the Misbegotten* is produced.

1950   Son Eugene dies.

1953   O'Neill develops pneumonia and dies on November 27 in Boston.

1956   *Long Day's Journey into Night* is produced. Jose Quintero revives *The Iceman Cometh.*

1957   *A Touch of the Poet* is produced.

1958   *Hughie* is produced.

1962   *More Stately Mansions* is produced.

Contributors

HAROLD BLOOM, Sterling Professor of the Humanities at Yale University, is the author of *The Anxiety of Influence, Poetry and Repression,* and many other volumes of literary criticism. His forthcoming study, *Freud: Transference and Authority,* attempts a full-scale reading of all of Freud's major writings. A MacArthur Prize Fellow, he is general editor of five series of literary criticism published by Chelsea House.

DORIS V. FALK is Professor Emeritus of English at Rutgers University. In addition to her work on O'Neill, she has written a major volume on Lillian Hellman.

ROBERT BRUSTEIN is Professor of English at Harvard University and Artistic Director of the American Repertory Theatre. His books include *Seasons of Discontent, The Third Theater,* and *The Culture Watch: Essays on Theater and Society.*

RAYMOND WILLIAMS is a Fellow of Jesus College, Cambridge. His many books include *The Country and the City, Culture and Society, Marxism and Literature,* and *Keywords.*

TIMO TIUSANEN, Professor of Theatre Research at the University of Helsinki, is the author of *O'Neill's Scenic Images,* and *Dürrenmatt, A Study in Plays, Prose, Theory.*

EGIL TÖRNQVIST has written widely on modern drama. His best-known books are *A Drama of Souls* and *Strindbergian Drama.*

TRAVIS BOGARD is Professor of Dramatic Art at the University of California, Berkeley. He is the author of *The Tragic Satire of John Webster* and volume 8, *American Drama,* of Ravel's *History of Drama in English.*

JEAN CHOTHIA is Assistant Lecturer in English at Selwyn College, Cambridge, and is the author of *Forging a Language.*

RICHARD B. SEWALL is Professor Emeritus of English at Yale University. He is the author of *The Vision of Tragedy* and *The Life of Emily Dickinson*.

JOHN ORR is Reader in Sociology at Edinburgh University where he also teaches English literature. He is author of two studies in modern tragedy, *Tragic Realism and Modern Society* and *Tragic Drama and Modern Society*. His most recent work is *The Making of the Twentieth Century Novel: Lawrence, Joyce, Faulkner and Beyond*.

C. W. E. BIGSBY is Reader in the School of English and American Studies at the University of East Anglia. He has edited *Superculture* and *Approach to Popular Culture*, and he is the author of *Confrontation and Commitment*, *Dada and Surrealism*, and *Tom Stoppard*.

Bibliography

Alexander, Doris M. *The Tempering of Eugene O'Neill*. New York: Harcourt, Brace & World, 1962.

Atkinson, Jennifer McCabe. *Eugene O'Neill: A Descriptive Bibliography*. University of Pittsburgh Press, 1974.

Bentley, Eric. "Trying to Like O'Neill." *Kenyon Review* 14 (July 1952): 476–92.

Berlin, Normand. *Eugene O'Neill*. New York: Grove, 1982.

Bigsby, C. W. E. *A Critical Introduction to Twentieth-Century American Drama, 1900–1940*, vol. 1. Cambridge: Cambridge University Press, 1982.

Bogard, Travis. *Contour in Time: The Plays of Eugene O'Neill*. New York: Oxford University Press, 1972.

Bowen, Croswell, with the assistance of Shane O'Neill. *The Curse of the Misbegotten: A Tale of the House of O'Neill*. New York: McGraw-Hill, 1959.

Broussard, Louis. *American Drama: Contemporary Allegory from Eugene O'Neill to Tennessee Williams*. Norman: University of Oklahoma Press, 1962.

Brustein, Robert. *The Theatre of Revolt*. Boston: Little, Brown, 1964.

Bryer, Jackson R. *Checklist of Eugene O'Neill*. Columbus, Ohio: Merrill, 1971.

———, ed. *"The Theatre We Worked For": The Letters of Eugene O'Neill to Kenneth Macgowan*. With introductory essays by Travis Bogard. New Haven: Yale University Press, 1982.

Cargill, Oscar, N. Bryllion Fagin, and William J. Fisher, eds. *O'Neill and His Plays: Four Decades of Criticism*. New York University Press, 1961.

Carpenter, Frederic I. *Eugene O'Neill*. Rev. ed. Boston: Twayne, 1979.

Chabrowe, Leonard. *Ritual and Pathos: The Theater of O'Neill*. Lewisburg, Pa.: Bucknell University Press, 1976.

Chiaromonte, Nicola. "Eugene O'Neill." *Sewanee Review* 68 (1960): 494–501.

Chothia, Jean. *Forging a Language: A Study of the Plays of Eugene O'Neill*. London: Cambridge University Press, 1979.

Clark, Barrett H. *Eugene O'Neill: The Man and His Plays*. Rev. ed. New York: Dover, 1947.

Driver, Tom F. "On the Later Plays of Eugene O'Neill." *Tulane Drama Review* 3 (December 1958): 8–20.

Engel, Edwin A. *The Haunted Heroes of Eugene O'Neill*. Cambridge: Harvard University Press, 1953.

Falk, Doris V. *Eugene O'Neill and the Tragic Tension: An Interpretive Study of the Plays*. New Brunswick, N.J.: Rutgers University Press, 1958.

Floyd, Virginia. *The Plays of Eugene O'Neill: A New Assessment*. New York: Frederick Ungar, 1985.

Frenz, Horst. *Eugene O'Neill*. Translated by Helen Sebba. New York: Frederick Ungar, 1971.

————, and Susan Tuck, eds. *Eugene O'Neill's Critics: Voices from Abroad*. Carbondale: Southern Illinois University Press, 1984.

Gassner, John. *Eugene O'Neill*. Minneapolis: University of Minnesota Press, 1965.

————, ed. *O'Neill: A Collection of Critical Essays*. Englewood Cliffs, N.J.: Prentice-Hall, 1964.

Gelb, Arthur, and Barbara Gelb. *O'Neill*. Enlarged ed. New York: Harper & Row, 1973.

Griffin, Ernest G., ed. *Eugene O'Neill: A Collection of Criticism*. New York: McGraw-Hill, 1976.

Leech, Clifford. *Eugene O'Neill*. New York: Grove, 1963.

Long, Chester Clayton. *The Role of Nemesis in the Structure of Selected Plays by Eugene O'Neill*. The Hague: Mouton, 1968.

McDonald, David. "The Phenomenology of the Glance in *Journey*." *Theatre Journal* 31 (October 1979): 343–56.

Manheim, Michael. *Eugene O'Neill's New Language of Kinship*. Syracuse University Press, 1982.

Martine, James J., ed. *Critical Essays on Eugene O'Neill*. Boston: G. K. Hall, 1984.

Miller, Jordan Y. *Eugene O'Neill and the American Critic: A Bibliographical Checklist*. 2d ed. rev. Hamden, Conn.: Archon, 1973.

————. *Playwright's Progress: O'Neill and the Critics*. Chicago: Scott, Foresman, 1965.

Moleski, Joseph J. "Eugene O'Neill and the Cruelty of Theater." *Comparative Drama* 15 (1982): 327–42.

Mottram, Eric. "Men and Gods: A Study of Eugene O'Neill." *Encore* 10, no.5 (September-October 1963): 26–44.

Orlandello, John. *O'Neill on Film*. Madison, N.J.: Fairleigh Dickinson University Press, 1982.

Raleigh, John Henry. "O'Neill's *Long Day's Journey into Night* and New England Irish-Catholicism." *Partisan Review* 26 (1959): 573–92.

————. *The Plays of Eugene O'Neill*. Carbondale: Southern Illinois University Press, 1965.

Ranald, Margaret Loftus. *The Eugene O'Neill Companion*. Westport, Conn.: Greenwood, 1984.

Reaver, J. Russell. *An O'Neill Concordance*. 3 vols. Detroit: Gale Research Co., 1969.

Redford, Grant H. "Dramatic Art vs. Autobiography: A Look at *Long Day's Journey into Night*." *College English* 25 (1964): 527–35.

Rich, J. Dennis. "Exile Without Remedy: The Late Plays of Eugene O'Neill." In *Eugene O'Neill: A World View*, edited by Virginia Floyd, 257–76. New York: Frederick Ungar, 1979.

Robinson, James A. *Eugene O'Neill and Oriental Thought: A Divided Vision*. Carbondale: Southern Illinois University Press, 1982.

————, and Eugene D. Shapiro. "The Defense of Psychoanalysis in Literature: *Journey* and *A View from the Bridge*." *Comparative Drama* 7 (Spring 1973): 51–67.

Sewall, Richard B. *The Vision of Tragedy*. New enlarged ed. New Haven: Yale University Press, 1980.

Shawcross, John T. "The Road to Ruin: The Beginning of O'Neill's *Journey*." *Modern Drama* 3 (1960): 289–96.

Sheaffer, Louis. *O'Neill: Son and Artist*. Boston: Little, Brown, 1973.

———. *O'Neill: Son and Playwright*. Boston: Little, Brown, 1968.

Sinha, C. P. *Eugene O'Neill's Tragic Vision*. Atlantic Highlands, N.J.: Humanities Press, 1981.

Stamm, Rudolf. "'Faithful Realism': Eugene O'Neill and the Problem of Style." *English Studies* 40, no. 4 (August 1959): 242–50.

Tiusanen, Timo. *O'Neill's Scenic Images*. Princeton University Press, 1968.

Törnqvist, Egil. *A Drama of Souls: Studies in O'Neill's Supernaturalistic Technique*. New Haven: Yale University Press, 1969.

———. "Strindberg and O'Neill." In *Structures of Influence: A Comparative Approach to August Strindberg*, edited by Marilyn J. Blackwell, 277–91. Chapel Hill: University of North Carolina Press, 1981.

Waith, Eugene M. "Eugene O'Neill: An Exercise in Unmasking." *Educational Theatre Journal* 13 (October 1961): 182–91. Reprinted in *O'Neill: A Collection of Critical Essays*, edited by John Gassner, 29–41.

Weissman, Philip. "Conscious and Unconscious Autobiographical Dramas of Eugene O'Neill." *Journal of the American Psychoanalytic Association* 5 (July 1957): 432–60.

Williams, Raymond. *Drama from Ibsen to Brecht*. New York: Oxford University Press, 1968.

Winther, Sophus Keith. *Eugene O'Neill: A Critical Study*. 2d ed., enlarged. New York: Russell & Russell, 1961.

Acknowledgments

"Long Day's Journey" by Doris V. Falk from *Eugene O'Neill and the Tragic Tension: An Interpretive Study of the Plays* by Doris V. Falk, © 1958 by Rutgers, The State University. Reprinted by permission of Rutgers University Press.

"The Theatre of Revolt: An Approach to Modern Drama" (originally entitled "Eugene O'Neill" by Robert Brustein from *The Theatre of Revolt: An Approach to Modern Drama* by Robert Brustein, © 1964 by Robert Brustein. Reprinted by permission of the author and Little, Brown & Company, in association with The Atlantic Monthly Press.

"*Long Day's Journey Into Night*: Eugene O'Neill" (originally entitled "Six Plays") by Raymond Williams from *Drama from Ibsen to Brecht* by Raymond Williams, © 1952, 1968 by Raymond Williams. Reprinted by permission of the author and Chatto & Windus Ltd.

"Through the Fog into the Monologue" by Timo Tiusanen from *O'Neill's Scenic Images* by Timo Tiusanen, © 1968 by Timo Tiusanen. Reprinted by permission of the author and Princeton University Press.

"Life in Terms of Lives" by Egil Törnqvist from *A Drama of Souls: Studies in O'Neill's Super-Naturalistic Technique* by Egil Törnqvist, © 1968 by Egil Törnqvist. Reprinted by permission of Yale University Press.

"The Door and the Mirror" by Travis Bogard from *Contour in Time: The Plays of Eugene O'Neill* by Travis Bogard, © 1972 by Oxford University Press. Reprinted by permission.

"Significant Form: *Long Day's Journey into Night*" by Jean Chothia from *Forging a Language: A Study of the Plays of Eugene O'Neill* by Jean Chothia, © 1979 by Cambridge University Press. Reprinted by permission.

"*Long Day's Journey into Night*" by Richard B. Sewall from *The Vision of Tragedy* (New Edition, Enlarged) by Richard B. Sewall, © 1980 by Yale University. Reprinted by permission of Yale University Press.

"Eugene O'Neill II: The Life Remembered" by John Orr from *Tragic Drama and Modern Society: Studies in the Social and Literary Theory of Drama from 1870 to the Present* by John Orr, © 1981 by John Orr. Reprinted by permission of the author, Macmillan Press Ltd., and Barnes & Noble Books, Totowa, New Jersey.

"The Retreat Behind Language" (originally entitled "Eugene O'Neill") by C. W. E. Bigsby from *A Critical Introduction to Twentieth-Century American Drama, 1900–1940*, vol. 1, by C. W. E. Bigsby, © 1982 by Cambridge University Press. Reprinted by permission.

Index